The Art of Connection:

The Secret Life of Sentences

Dr Ian McCormick

Published by Quibble Academic

Copyright © 2013 Ian McCormick

All rights reserved.

ISBN: 1493748416
ISBN-13: 978-1493748419

DEDICATION

To all my students 1991-2013.

CONTENTS

Acknowledgements	i
1 Introduction	3
1.1 The Social Sentence	3
1.2 The Use of Connection	9
1.3 Understanding the Psychology of Transition	13
1.4 Style, Oratory, Elegance	17
1.5 The flow of spontaneity and passion	20
1.6 Power, Rhetoric and Repetition	24
1.7 The Philosophy of Association	29
1.8 Beyond the Logic of Connection	31
1.9 *Écriture feminine*	34
1.10 Openings: the genesis of this book	37
2. The Art of Location	41
3. The Art of Timing	51
4. The Art of Comparison	73
5. The Art of Contrast and Difference	87
6. The Art of the Supplement	101
7. The Art of Disputation	109
8. The Art of the Sequence	115
9. The Art of Example and Illustration	129
10. The Art of the Summary	141
11. Further Reading	149
About the Author	159

ACKNOWLEDGMENTS

The Art of Connection was written primarily to support students who were working in the English language. In fact, my research was grounded in my experience of working in education during the last twenty-five years. For many of those years I worked as an academic tutor in Higher Education – in the University sector. In more recent years I have served as a tutor working with a variety of international students from Asia, Eastern Europe, and the Middle East. In the course of these different kinds of work my knowledge of how language works gained from working directly with students at different levels across a range of different subjects; from social media to medicine, from the arts to engineering, from technology to statistics and biochemistry. I frequently found that students experience difficult with the structure and with the organisation of their ideas. Through working with children I realised that the arts of connection and transition were the building blocks for written composition, for effective speechmaking, and for the development of rational discourse. The primary dedication of this book is therefore to the creative engagement that I have enjoyed with my students over the years.

But scholarship also requires practical resources. My research for this book would not have been possible without the support of several key libraries and their helpful staff throughout Great Britain. I am therefore grateful to the libraries and their staff at the University of St Andrews, the University of Leeds, and the University of Birmingham. The central library of the City of Birmingham, and the Smethwick Branch Library in Sandwell, also assisted me with many enquiries and requests.

Most significantly I am deeply grateful to Dr Iain G. Armstrong for his support and encouragement in this project; for his design skills, creative flair, and for his dedicated and constructive work in the final stages of proof-reading. Without him, the publication of this book would not have been possible.

'Only connect! That was the whole of her sermon. Only connect the prose and the passion, and both will be exalted, and human love will be seen at its highest.'

--- E. M. Forster, *Howard's End*.

'Hereby I learned have, not to despise,
What ever thing seems small in common eyes.'

--- Edmund Spenser, *Visions of the World's Vanity*

Ian McCormick

1. INTRODUCTION

1.1 The Social Sentence

This book is the first comprehensive compendium of the most common connective and transitional words. In addition, this book provides examples of the art of transition drawn from a range of published texts. Although the number of different ways to start a sentence is infinite, there are many customary and common variations that writers choose as openings. Moreover, these words are selected with a high degree of frequency because they support the flow of ideas. As these words are quite common we tend not to notice them consciously as we read. Yet these transitions and connective words play a key role because they facilitate the process of writing and reading. They work at the level of thought and they work at the level of feeling. They help our creative and critical thoughts to flow more effectively. Accordingly, it seems reasonable to assume that the art of the connection is at the centre of all thinking and writing. At times, the flow of thought also signal breaks and new directions. In other words, we make and mark the moment of transition by means of distinction and disconnection, as much as by similarity and likeness.

In a real sense, sentences enjoy a social life; they flow into one another. In part, this phenomenon is the product of the flow of ideas. Clearly, there is a stream of consciousness at work in our writing, as much as in our day-dreaming. And artists often work quite hard to produce the desired sense of smooth transition. Or to break it, for effect and impact. Writing has the quality of flow when there is a sense of vital association running beneath the impressions. While the movement of ideas may appear to be natural, or inevitable, it is in fact a highly constructed process. For this reason, one aspect of the craft of writing involves learning how to use connective words or phrases, and also knowing when to avoid them. Judicious use of transitional words can be very effective, but excessive use tends to sound either awkward, artificial, or robotic. The art is, in some degree, a case of concealing the art: *ars est celare artem*. By making choices we are exercising our sense of critical and aesthetic judgment. In practice, writers tend to evolve a crafted style that is also their unique style, it has their stamp on it. Sometimes styles can be quite individualistic or idiosyncratic; they bear the stamp of their author's voice and sensibility. At other times writers want to communicate effectively in a more neutral way and that objective will often entail being more objective and less personal in approach. In academic essays and discourse we want the ideas and the logic to shine through. But in the case of persuasive writing rhetorical techniques are often used, and the *persona* or personality of the writer will be a constructed, trusted and credible effect of the writing. Writers do not just *express*; they *create* identities.

Most writers are familiar with the idea that the style of writing needs to match the purpose of the composition. Most writers sense that there is a time for poetry and for rhetorical devices, but there is also a time for plain, unaffected style that does not draw attention to its gaudy artistry, its ornate elegance, its excessive use of textbook rhetorical devices. But techniques are seldom purely transparent to the more alert readers, or to the trained critic. Ideally there is a subtle interplay between the form, the content and the style of the writing. For inexperienced writers this supple and subtle combination of forces is quite difficult to achieve. Clearly, the craft of writing may be learned, but the art of writing is often elusive, and difficult even to define, let alone create on the page. Increasingly, teachers have been identifying the failure of students to join up their ideas effectively in their compositions. The authors of *Successful Academic Writing*, for instance, have recently noted that 'Students often struggle to provide adequate links between sentences.' Crucially, they have also rightly asserted that 'This problem can be overcome easily.' (2009: 105). The purpose of this book is both to meet that challenge and to show the copious variety that the English language affords the writer in dealing with these difficulties.

We tend to think of sentences as self-standing units of sense;

they are comprehensible in isolation. Typically, grammarians analyse how a sentence functions. They *parse* a sentence as a single unit of meaning, as the exemplification of rules at work. Moreover, children learn to create simple, and then more complex sentences, progressively. But we have always attended too much in teaching and learning to the unit of meaning at the level of the sentence.

In fact, the pleasure of writing and reading springs from the connective tissue of language, and from the effectiveness of transitional words that allow sentences to flow *together* as a dialogue. The relationship between sentences is not a grammatical relation. The relationship between sentences crosses over into the field of creative narrative, on the one hand, and philosophy, on the other. The relationship between sentences is at the core of storytelling and it is the equivalent in philosophy of the different kinds of relationship observed in logic. Obviously, sloppy, weak and confused sentences are disastrous. But my focus in this book is really more on meaning and relationship as the total effect of the combinations of intertwined sentences. The emphasis will be more on the complete organic work, or at least the paragraph, rather than the isolated fragment or the solitary stand-alone sentence. Connective words and transition phrases provide the text with a body that functions as an organic unit rather than as lifeless, chopped-up body parts. In particular, connectives help to hold ideas together at the level of the paragraph. Although style guides often explain how to structure an essay by using topic sentences to introduce a key theme or concept, the internal paragraph links between sentences benefit from close scrutiny. In this regard, Edward H. Grout usefully observed in his book *Standard English: Structure and Style* that

> The true unit of composition is the paragraph. Although the old definition of a sentence was: a complete thought expressed in words, a sentence very seldom does express a complete thought. There is in most sentences an over-current or under-current of thought that is mingled with preceding or subsequent sentences. In perspicuous writing the flow of thought is apparent and unmistakable. (1933: 94)

Traditionally, the study of grammar and the practice of composition have primarily emphasised the role of the sentence. By shifting the focus to transition and connection we engage the heart and the mind in the production of paragraphs. We attend more to the rhythm of the sentence and to the flow of associated thoughts. Again Edward H. Grout has outlined the benefits of this approach:

> By the appropriate use of pronouns, repetitions, and connectives the continuity of the composition is maintained, and the reader is able to follow the writer's thought with ease. It is almost as important that the meaning of a writer should be clear as that it should be correct, for clarity of form is an aid to clarity of thinking. (1933: 94)

In his book *Style*, F. L. Lucas described a model sentence that is 'fine in sense, and fine in rhythm, and easy to articulate – not congested with consonants nor disfigured by jingles.' But he also understood this musicality as a flow, offering his readers the picture of electric transmission: 'Think of meanings (*and associations*) of a group of words as an electric current; of their sounds as the conductor. Some conduct better than others; some offer marked resistance.' But he warns against the supersensitivity of a writer or critic who becomes obsessed with the nuances, the finer vibrations of prose style: 'The whole business is liable to degenerate into mere foppery and frippery.' (1955: 250) In this regard we are reminded on the contrast between Edmund Burke's ornate oratory deployed to denounce the French Revolution and Thomas Paine's pithy defence of transformation endowed with the vibrant energy of the vernacular. The ideological battle symptomatically was also fought and thought with words – the weapons of communication. For Tom Paine, Burke's use of the sentence was a version of the old order, traditional, lifeless and backward looking:

> How dry, barren, and obscure is the source from which Mr. Burke labours! and how ineffectual, though gay with flowers, are all his declamation and his arguments compared with these clear, concise, and soul-animating sentiments! Few and short as they are, they lead on to a vast field of generous and manly thinking, and do not finish, like Mr. Burke's periods, with music in the ear, and nothing in the heart. (*The Rights of Man*, 1791).

When flow of sentences is closely observed we notice that new ideas are constantly pushing out of and away from the earlier ones. In this process there is an elusive element of play at work as meaning shifts along a chain of connection. In a crucial sense, a sentence supplements its precursor, but is also supplants it. Meaning is less the effect of a specific sentence, but rather more deconstructively, it is an effect that flows across the textual surface in the process of reading. By crafting transitions the writer aims to regulate the sense of direction. By providing helpful signposts the goal aimed at is clarity and lucidity, rather than the natural muddle of absolute spontaneity and isolated fragments. By learning the art of transition all aspects of communication will be improved.

The desired balance between complex writing and free flowing speech, and between artificiality and natural flow, is a constant issue in the art of composition. Obviously, the style of the writer is affected by character and context, by the society or culture, and by the subject matter. In this regard, textbooks in rhetoric and composition traditionally offered rules and recommendations, but there is also the sense of an essential relationship at some level between art and life, between the learned activity of communication and its native or natural pulse. These tensions are valuable and they cannot be fully eradicated, nor ought they to be. In his popular book *Elements of Criticism* (1762) Lord Kames observed that 'the genuine rules of criticism are all of them derived from the human heart.' Similarly, in his *Essay on Criticism* (1711) the poet Alexander Pope famously announced that

> Those rules of old discovered, not devised,
> Are nature still, but nature methodized:
> Nature, like liberty, is but restrained
> By the same laws which first herself ordained.

So it appears that excellent writing, even the classical rhetorical writing so admired in the eighteenth century, is a successful marriage between freedom and restraint. Sentences can be joined in happy union, but they may also have an independent life. More importantly, there is no point to the enforcement of rules for their own sake; they have their foundation in a delicate awareness of natural relations. In this regard it has been fascinating to observe that the most common school-learned rules, such as the one that declares that the word *And* should not be used to start sentences, do not stand up to scrutiny in terms of common use by respected literary writers. The research undertaken for his book provided countless examples of rules regarding the position within a sentence of 'and', or the embedding of 'however', and 'therefore' not being observed. Conversely, it was also noticeable that the transition words often sit most comfortably within a sentence, just after the opening, if we want them to be less obtrusive.

The broad objective of this book was to collect and describe common usage, rather than to prescribe a correct style suitable for all times, places and all occasions. Nonetheless, a familiarity with custom and tradition is an essential training for the apprentice writer. There is greater opportunity for subtle innovation after the common storehouse of the possibilities of the language has become second nature. After that, as Alexander Pope has declared, the greatest prize involves cautiously breaking the rules in order to achieve the more romantic effect of imaginative flight:

Thus Pegasus, a nearer way to take,
May boldly deviate from the common Track.
Great Wits sometimes may gloriously offend,
And rise to Faults true Criticks dare not mend;
From vulgar Bounds with brave Disorder part,
And snatch a Grace beyond the Reach of Art,
Which, without passing thro' the Judgment, gains
The Heart, and all its End at once attains.
In Prospects, thus, some Objects please our Eyes,
Which out of Nature's common Order rise,
The shapeless Rock, or hanging Precipice.

It must be conceded that connective and transitional words are not essential; they are by no means compulsory. Often it is better to leave them out, rather than stick them in abruptly and obtrusively. Most sentences run along happily without them. We should also be cautious not to use them excessively, or repetitively. But used with moderation, effective transitions serve as the ligaments of writing. Alternatively, this connective quality is like having glue that sticks sentences together. By making careful use of customary or conventional opening words and phrases in the composition of sentences we help to signal transitions. This process can be compared to travelers who benefit from reading sign-posts; these pointers inform the reader about the direction of the ideas; they help us to keep a sense of where we are. The use of this technique allows readers to have a smooth journey; they are less likely to feel lost. With the help of customary connective words the process of writing also becomes less arduous. By using transitional words prudently the writer's ideas will also be communicated with greater clarity, effectiveness and precision. But an excess of signposts is also distracting for the driver. And some journeys are more of a ramble in which there is a pleasure to be gained by not knowing where the path or track is leading us. These issues will be explored in greater detail below.

1.2 The Use of Connection

Before proceeding to more complex ideas the notion of *relationship* will be considered. Connective and transition words are the little unsung - and often wholly unnoticed - heroes of English composition. In summary, connective and transition words serve:

1. to provide a sense of *where* something is in relation to something else;
2. to supply a sense of *when* something is happening;
3. to compare two ideas and express *similarities*;
4. to contrast ideas. English provides many examples to signal the notion of *difference*;
5. to present additional or *supplementary* ideas;
6. to indicate that a point in a discussion has been *conceded* or already taken into account;
7. to demonstrate a sense of *logical sequence*;
8. to offer an *illustration* or an *example*;
9. to deliver a *summary* of the ideas discussed.

In more detail, connective and transition words...

1. Provide a sense of *where* something is in relation to something else. This use is rather like using a preposition or an adverbial phrase. The words associated with this usage are: above, across, adjacent, adjacent to, alongside, amid, among, around, at the side, away, at this point, before, behind, below, beneath, beside, between, beyond, down, from, further, here, here and there, in front of, in the back, in the background, in the center of, in the distance, in the foreground, in the front, in the middle, just outside, near, nearby, next, on the side, opposite to, over, there, to the left, to the right, to the side, under, up, where, wherever.. These words all suggest a sense of *place* or *location* and are therefore very useful for visual description.

2. Supply a sense of *when* something is happening, or to communicate the sense of a logical sequence in *time*. Examples of this usage of transitional words and phrases are: after, afterward, all of a sudden, as soon as, as often, at about, at last, at the present time, at the same time, at this instant, before, currently, during, earlier, ere long, eventually, even while, finally, first, formerly, forthwith, fourth, from time to time, henceforth, immediately, in a

moment, in due time, initially, in the first place, in the future, in the meantime, in the past, in time, instantly, last, later, meanwhile, next, now, occasionally, often, once, presently, prior to, quickly, second, shortly, since, sometimes, soon, sooner or later, straightaway, subsequently, suddenly, then, third, to begin with, today, until, until now, up to the present time, when, whenever, without delay.

3. Point to a *comparison* of two ideas. This may be achieved by deploying words such as additionally, again, also, and, as, as a matter of fact, as well as, by the same token, comparatively, correspondingly, coupled with, equally, equally important; furthermore, identically, in addition, in like manner, in the light of, in the same fashion, in the same way, like, likewise, moreover, not only ... but also, not to mention, of course, similarly, to say nothing of, together with, too. As these examples demonstrate the ruling idea is *similarity*.

4. Indicate a *contrast*. English provides many examples to signal the notion of *difference*. The most common examples are: above all, after all, albeit, and still, and yet, although, although this may be true, at the same time, be that as it may, besides, but, conversely, despite, different from, even so, even though, however, in contrast, in reality, in spite of, instead, nevertheless, nonetheless, notwithstanding, on the contrary, on the other hand, or, otherwise, rather, regardless of, still, then again, unlike, whereas, while, yet.

5. If the writer wants to present additional or *supplementary* ideas the most common options are: additionally, admittedly, again, also, and, another reason, as well, besides, equally, furthermore, in addition, moreover, then again, too.

6. In the process of disputation, *argument,* or debate a writer sometimes indicates that a point has been agreed or already taken into account. In order to suggest that a point has been *conceded* the following words and phrases may be used: above all, chiefly, chief attribute, clearly, for the most part, more particularly, most curious, most significantly, generally, the general truth, to be more precise.

7. In order to provide a sense of *logical sequence* the writer uses

words such as accordingly, as a result, because, because of, consequently, due to, even if, for fear that, for this reason, for the purpose of, forthwith, granted (that), hence, henceforth, if, in case, in order to, in that case, in the event that, in the hope that, in view of, inasmuch as, lest, on account of, on (the) condition (that), only, owing to, provided that, seeing that, since, so, so as to, so long as, so that, thereby, therefore, thereupon, thus, to the end that, under those circumstances, unless, when, whenever, while, with this in mind, with this intention. In these examples there may be a sense of cause and effect, or the sense that one idea results from another. In some cases there is the sense of *conditionality* or a specific relation of *purpose*.

8. If the writer has been using concepts, ideas, or theories, it is often helpful to provide an *illustration* or an *example*. For this purpose we deploy words such as: another point, as an illustration, chiefly, especially, first thing to remember, for example, for instance, for one thing, for this reason, frequently, important to realize, in detail, in fact, in general, in other words, in particular, in this case, indeed, like, issues to consider, markedly, must be remembered, namely, notably, point often overlooked, recalling, specifically, such as, surely, surprisingly, that is to say, taking into account, to be sure, to put it another way, to put it differently, to repeat, with reference to, with regard to, with this in mind.

9. Finally, we may wish to signal that we are offering a *summary* of our ideas. In this regard useful connective words include: after all, all in all, all things considered, by and large, finally, for the most part, generally speaking, hence, in a word, in any event, in brief, in conclusion, in conclusion, in essence, in fact, in short, in summary, in the final analysis, in the long run, on balance, on the whole, ordinarily, overall, that is to say, that is, to sum up, to summarize, usually.

It will be clear that many transitional words have multiple and overlapping functions. The summary, for instance, also signals the end of a sequence. Similarly, examples may also be supplements, because they provide additional illustrations or instances. The mobility of these words ought to be understood as one of their strengths. They have evolved to express practical movements in time and space, as well as to serve the more abstract needs of deeper thought and critical reflection.

At this stage, the enthusiastic reader has the option to jump directly into later sections of the book. The later sections arrange the most common words and phrases in conceptual groups. This approach therefore demonstrates the variety of options for connection and illustrates this resource by providing examples drawn from published sources. It is hoped that this strategy will be useful both to native speakers at many levels of education and development, as well as to those other speakers learning to write English for the first time. It is recommended that readers sample the book by dipping into it periodically. After that, it is worth observing closely the use of connection in the texts that you come across. As you become more familiar with the correct usage it is then a simple process to begin to select and use some of the examples in your own work. But again, it is important to sound a cautionary note: sentences should not be too sticky, and connectives should not stick out too obtrusively. It is wise, therefore, to aim for judicious deployment, rather than intrusive engagement. Having become more sensitive to the craft of connection, the next stage will be to achieve a mastery of disconnection. In the art of transition we must learn to accept, and know when to decline. There is more to style than smooth and harmonious transitions.

If you want to think more profoundly about the process of connection the remainder of this introduction offers a broader outline of the underlying topic of transitional processes from a variety of perspectives, within the wider contexts of different theories of rhetoric and composition.

Looking back: does *this* idea make sense? One of the most common ways to join sentences in academic writing is to deploy a modest word such as *This*. But sentences beginning 'this means that' can be rather clumsy and pedestrian. There is a risk that *this* is unclear in terms of *what* is being designated from the foregoing discussion. Therefore it may be helpful to use an appropriate abstract noun in order to clarify the sense, and in order to emphasise the primacy of rational discourse. In this regard, common words are:

account, advice, answer, argument, area, assertion, assumption, claim, comment, concept, conclusion, confusion, contradiction, criticism, critique, decrease, description, deterioration, difficulty, discussion, distinction, drawback, effect, emphasis, error, estimate, example, explanation, failing, finding, hypothesis, idea, improvement, increase, interpretation, narrative, notion, observation, paradigm, proof, proposal, reading, reference, report, setback, situation, strategy, suggestion, tactic, theory, variation, view, warning, weakness.

If the writer has a solid grounding in these words then new sentences can be constructed with facility and swiftness:

> This strategy has the virtue of simplicity.
> This description is muddled.
> This narrative is disconnected.
> This discussion has reached a conclusion.

At other times, *This* will be replaced with the name of the attributed author, as in these examples,

> Strawson's reading of analytical philosophy is fundamentally flawed.
>
> Russell's account of the Western tradition has some weaknesses.
>
> Newton's theories have been modified by new research in recent years.

So, it turns out that with a little support, this technique will be easy to implement in your writing and speaking. With the greater emphasis now placed on exams, it is increasingly important to have a ready-made bank of phrases that will allow the writer to express ideas with clarity and celerity and cogency. In a pressured environment the writer who has ready-made sentence openers to hand escapes the tyranny of the blank page. Sentences begin to mirror the flow of ideas; they propagate by virtue of their relationships, rather than sticking out as awkward, isolated units. By working with sentence openers and transitional phrases the writer is less likely to suffer from writer's block.

1.3 Understanding the Psychology of Transition

By becoming more conscious of how writers use connective words we begin to learn by example how to use them appropriately. At an early stage in child development transitions begin to appear in the learned use of language. After that emergence we begin to witness the emergence of more complex thought patterns. Less familiar forms of transitions are also less frequent, and they may only be present in written texts, or be deployed solely in highly formal speech situations. In fact, some forms of transition and connection are chiefly limited to particular professions such as academic philosophy or jurisprudence.

If you have shared the pleasure of working with young children, you will be familiar with the developmental stage of speaking when all phrases are joined by the connective word 'and'. This process of social and interactive learning leads, typically, to the adoption of 'then' as the word chosen to express the description of events or thoughts in a sequence. After a period of time the child learns more complex modes of transition because the capacity for more complex sequence and abstraction is also tied into a process of progressive cognitive development.

But there is more at stake than the child's basic familiarity with a set of desirable words: connectives help to show that a process of reasoning is taking place, and that this can be communicated to others in a meaningful fashion. In fact, the confident deployment of connectives provides evidence for the emergence of cognitive complexity and it is an early marker for intellectual development. Typically, in the field of education one of the learning objectives will be to assist children to adopt a sufficiently wide variety of connectives to present different perspectives effectively. In this regard, the ability to think, and competence with connectives and openers, are intertwined. Having connecting options to hand allows the speaker or writer to consciously reflect on the next step in a line of argument. In other words, logical connectives help the lines of thought to flow efficiently and effectively. The process of social interaction based on questions and answers is also significant in forming a chain of connection. In this context, Louis Bloom has argued that

> The confident use of such words suggests that the child has grasped the value of an unfolding discourse in which relations of coherence need to be established. By responding to questions such as 'Why?' children also begin to employ connectives such as 'because' and in the process demonstrate that they are able to communicate a sense of causality. By asking 'why' questions children also gain from others the experience of hearing how connectives such as 'because' mark out the answer to a query. The reported research findings suggest that this stage of child development that shows the appearance of 'why' questions typically occurs at 30 months of age. (1993: 367)

Nonetheless, there is a risk in asserting absolute transcultural linguistic generalisations. In their discussion of 'Structures beyond the Sentence' in *Grammar and Writing* Rebecca Stott and Kim Landers offer some useful qualifications to the general position on logical connection and grammar:

> Coherence is the first essential in a text, a recognizable structure of thought and ideas. It is created partly by the writer or speaker, but also by the reader or listener, who responds to the signals given by the text. Because of this double nature, coherence is a complex matter to analyse, though it is not difficult to produce. It depends on a context of culture, attitudes and knowledge which aren't always consciously recognised or shared by the producer or by its audience. (2001: 128)

In a wider sense, these types of linguistic, grammatical or logical competence in adults may also support confident expression because they build on the efficient management of ideas (structure) and the use of effective communication (styles of delivery). Increasingly, business people are using the visualisation of connected thinking and connective intelligence in order to improve leadership, communication and productivity in the workplace. Business and social networks also employ the broader discourse of follower, following, connecting and linking. As we are frequently told, we are living in a connected world. The psychology of connection is a valued commodity in business and social media, and in the social media business. But these are wider issues and they are beyond the scope of this book.

Returning to the field of educational psychology, it is not uncommon to enter a primary or elementary school classroom that displays giant posters of 'the connective pyramid.' At the apex is 'and.' Below that we are likely to meet up with our old friends: but, so, then, because, when. After that we move into a zone where spoken and more literary forms begin to operate. In this zone are words such as although, however, also, even though, besides, if, as well as, after, while, nevertheless. After that the connectives and openers are clearly more literary, and less frequently used in spoken English. These formal acquaintances include: in addition to, on the contrary. And beyond these words, the discourse starts to sound highly specialised; with the frequent occurrence of *whereas*, or *notwithstanding*, we may be urged to take up litigation, or we may just fail to read the small print of the legal disclaimer.

Nowadays teachers work very hard with learners to help them acquire a consciousness of different connective words. At a higher level of linguistic competence the aim will be to foster the confident deployment of a range of suitable sentence openers. The evidence that these words or phrases are being used will in turn contribute to the teacher's positive evaluation of the learner's work. The most common connectives give way in time to the confident deployment of a range of sentence openers that help ideas to flow logically, or enable them to work as a coherent narrative. Indeed, the effective use of literary style is the hallmark of civilized writing. At a higher level learners begin to identify and deploy rhetorical techniques such as the triple repetition of words and phrases. At this point an element of restraint may be required because the frequent use of the most common connectives starts to sound mechanical. By drawing attention to themselves the connectives bite back; their partial invisibility becomes a monstrous presence that obstructs the flow of ideas. Rather than being helpful signposts, we crash into them.

If we think of our life as composed of sentences, then we begin to discern the essential role of composition in making sense of the moment, as well as in constructing our larger narratives of meaning. Alternatively, let us entertain the notion that life is the question and you are the answer. Or to reverse the calling, you are the answer to one or more of life's questions. The marvellous art of connection stops your life from falling into chaos. At one level sentences touch and join; at another level, people connect and follow common interests. As we have been noting above, the art of connection starts early in the child's social and intellectual development. This developmental process continues to progress throughout life, and even lives on beyond our death insofar as our words and deeds will have touched people, and may still connect with the living in a memorable way.

In the course of writing, the processing of words is learned again as the awareness of an inner voice, the inner compulsion to connect. As adults, we often forget the foundational role of connection because we have taken it for granted and we have become lazy or sloppy in our use of connection. Yet we can re-learn connection by becoming more alert to its value. With judicious use of effective connections, and with the deployment of a range of fresh openings, the English language begins to work for us; by making friends with language we gain opportunities for creative engagement and we sharpen the use of our capacity for critical insight. In our rush to embrace future technologies we have forgotten, perhaps, to engage with the most marvellous and astonishing technology: the technology of the word. By connecting sentences we make more sense out of the words and the world. We transition between the two more effectively.

1.4 Style, Oratory, Elegance

Although this is not the place to explore in any historical depth the relationship between style, oratory and elegant writing, it is essential to understand that there is an underlying and healthy conflict between highly artificial modes of expression and the preference for natural speech, unadorned discourse and a more improvisational approach to composition. In part this description betrays a false dichotomy, since the use of written language, or the delivery of a formal speech, is 'always-already' reliant on of a high degree of learned technique. Therefore, the return to a pure state of nature is nothing more than a romantic delusion. There are degrees of techniques and artificiality rather than none at all. Except in very young infants, language use is far more than a stream of random or experimental babble.

Nonetheless, at the other extreme, the idea of a purely logical or philosophical language was one of the aspirations of seventeenth century thinkers such as John Wilkins (1614-1672). In *An Essay towards a Real Character and a Philosophical Language* (1668) he was seeking to outline a plan for a universal language. This was a recurring dream of the Enlightenment, but it quickly comes up against the loose viscosity of conventional speech situations. Most famously, the notion that there might be an direct relationship between the word and the thing, and that we might establish a universal language, was a topic satirized by Jonathan Swift (1667-1745) in his grotesque and ridiculous depiction of the Professors at work in the Grand Academy of Lagado in the Third Book of *Gulliver's Travels* (1726). When it comes to systems of language and hard rules of style, we ought to maintain a healthy degree of scepticism. The academic critical methodology runs the risk of destructive examination. As the romantic writer Samuel Taylor Coleridge (1772-1834) noted,

> Sweet is the lore which Nature brings;
> Our meddling intellect
> Mis-shapes the beauteous forms of things: ---

We murder to dissect.

The romantic perspective was a manifesto against the main trend of scientific enlightenment that was underway at the end the seventeenth century. The Royal Society (established in 1660) had taken as its motto *Nullius in verba* (Take nobody's word for it) and required the language of experimentation to be a 'bare report of Matter of Fact.' This approach entailed the rejection of 'Prefaces, Apologies, or Rhetorical Flourishes.' Accordingly, scientific and medical writers increasingly aimed to adopt the plain language of modernity while the cultural sphere insisted on the classical tradition of rhetoric, which was derived from antiquity. In part, there was an emergent class difference in the eighteenth century, between the civilization of the aristocracy and the grubby hands of the new middle class experimentalists. At risk of simplifying complex and contradictory trends, it might be stated that the tension between plain speech and florid, noble elegance begins to be more apparent after the seventeenth century. Moreover, the emergent popular forms of cultural production, such as the early novel and journalism, begin to adopt a less formal, less classical style. But these popular literary innovations were, nonetheless, regarded as low or degenerate forms; as Grub Street rather than polite Country House discourse.

The significance and value of literary style was most eloquently expressed by Lord Chesterfield (1694–1773) in his *Letters to his Son*:

> Style is the dress of thoughts; and let them be ever so just, if your style is homely, coarse, and vulgar, they will appear to as much disadvantage, and be as ill received as your person, though ever so well proportioned, would, if dressed in rags, dirt, and tatters. It is not every understanding that can judge of matter; but every ear can and does judge more or less of style; and were I either to speak or write to the public, I should prefer moderate matter, adorned with all the beauties and elegancies of style, to the strongest matter in the world, ill-worded and ill-delivered.

The notion that social class and literary style are intertwined will be clear from this quotation. But the writer also noted that style may be acquired; it is not a birthright, nor is it a natural inheritance. In order to achieve greatness the writer should learn from the example of the best writing available: 'he need only attend to, observe, and imitate the best authors.' Incidentally, this comment provides a rationale in this book for the extensive use of examples drawn from published writing across a variety of fields: from the arts and sciences, from medicine and law, and from the social sciences. The aim was to demonstrate that rhetorical technique, logical thought and clear expression operate across many domains and discourse fields. Scientific and philosophical writing is just as heavily restricted by the dictates of a formal style as the discourse of a racy fictional romance is by its conventions, traditions and reader-expectations.

For Lord Chesterfield the reputation of a gentleman was directly and significantly related to the care taken with language use. Importantly, he identified effective writing and rhetorical accomplishment in speech as a *learned* activity:

> It is a very true saying, that a man must be born a poet, but that he may make himself an orator; and the very first principle of an orator is, to speak his own language, particularly, with the utmost purity and elegance. A man will be forgiven, even great errors, in a foreign language; but in his own even the least slips are justly laid hold of and ridiculed. [...] I must repeat it to you over and over again, that with all the knowledge which you may have at present or hereafter acquire, and with all the merit that ever man had, if you have not a graceful address, liberal and engaging manners, a prepossessing air, and a good degree of eloquence in speaking and writing, you will be nobody; but will have the daily mortification of seeing people, with not one-tenth part of your merit or knowledge, get the start of you and disgrace you both in company and in business.

I suspect that there are few 'How to Get Ahead in Business' conduct books that echo the emphasis placed by Lord Chesterfield's on the adoption of a fitting and suitable style. Yet the recurring complaint from the business world is one that laments the poor expression of entrepreneurs and the muddled messages of its leaders. In an increasingly collaborative, team-driven environment, the value of connection, connectivity and connectedness are highly valued characteristics. Whether social or business connection starts with a thought or an emotion, it has its roots in language. By investing in language we will reap rich rewards.

1.5 The flow of spontaneity and passion

There is, nonetheless, a tradition that is contrary to the studied elegance of Lord Chesterfield's rhetoric. The romantic opposition tends to privilege the spontaneity of flow, passion and improvisation. In literary terms, the inability of logical language to capture the life of a person was whimsically explored by Laurence Sterne (1713-1768) in his novel *The Life and Opinions of Tristram Shandy, Gentleman*. One of his characteristic techniques was the use of the dash to capture the swift transitions of dialogue and thought in motion:

> The Homunculus, Sir, in however low and ludicrous a light he may appear, in this age of levity, to the eye of folly or prejudice;—to the eye of reason in scientific research, he stands confess'd—a Being guarded and circumscribed with rights.—The minutest philosophers, who by the bye, have the most enlarged understandings, (their souls being inversely as their enquiries) shew us incontestably, that the Homunculus is created by the same hand,—engender'd in the same course of nature,—endow'd with the same locomotive powers and faculties with us:—That he consists as we do, of skin, hair, fat, flesh, veins, arteries, ligaments, nerves, cartilages, bones, marrow, brains, glands, genitals, humours, and articulations;—is a Being of as much activity,—and in all senses of the word, as much and as truly our fellow-creature as my Lord Chancellor of England.—He may be benefitted,—he may be injured,—he may obtain redress; in a word, he has all the claims and rights of humanity, which Tully, Puffendorf, or the best ethick writers allow to arise out of that state and relation.

The dashes support the flow as well as the sense of the ideas having an emotional urgency. Significantly, Laurence Sterne was influenced by John Locke's notion of the association of ideas, by the chains of cause and effect, and by erroneous linkages, digressions and winding paths that never reach their destination. As a result, Sterne's approach mimics the lack of sequence and order in real life. As a creative work his novel offers an exhilarating experience because the author simulates a closeness to the flow of thoughts and feelings. But this style also has its limitations because critical reflection often requires a distance from experience. Sterne's style therefore appears to impose a limit on rational communication as a project for life. As Anne K. Mellor noted in *English Romantic Irony*

> This is a novel that has no necessary form or causal connections. Hence it is a novel that barely gets written; a novel in which every character rides his own hobby horse, obsessed with ideas he cannot verbally communicate; a novel that finally suggests that the only way people can reach each other, if at all, is through emotions and sexuality and not through rational discourse. (1990: 4)

While this form and technique of writing is a brilliant creative experience, it is a risky strategy for the student of composition. In a chapter entitled 'The Essay Writing Process' Rebecca Stott delivers a helpful warning:

> However, Sterne's narrator, Tristram, never gets to the end of his story, even finds it impossible to begin, because 'there's no end of it' and he never finds a way of selecting out material. You, however, need to finish your essay in a specific period of time or you will fail. Your aim is to make an argument, not to show your reader, like Sterne, that life is complicated and impossible to write about. Consequently, you will need an order and you will need to select your material.

By capturing the natural vitality of the moment and the winding quest to make sense of what's happening in the moment, Laurence Sterne evolved a style that won admiration and delight as well as hostility from critics. The following quotation from the literary critic H. D. Traill demonstrates the degree of censure to which this species of writing has been subjected. It is also, after a fashion, an example of the rhetorical style employed as critical discourse. This example, in its turn, shows us the difference between serene study as critical reflection, and the complex emotional tangle of our feelings and passions, delivered as a chaotic or shifting *flow*:

> To talk of "the style" of Sterne is almost to play one of those tricks with language of which he himself was so fond. For there is hardly any definition of the word which can make it possible to describe him as having any style at all. It is not only that he manifestly recognised no external canons whereto to conform the expression of his thoughts, but he had apparently no inclination to invent and observe, except indeed in the most negative of senses, any style of his own. The "style of Sterne," in short, is as though one should say "the form of Proteus."

He was determined to be uniformly eccentric, regularly irregular, and that was all. His digressions, his "asides," and his fooleries, in general, would of course have in any case necessitated a certain jerkiness of manner; but this need hardly have extended itself habitually to the structure of individual sentences, and as a matter of fact he can at times write, as he does for the most part in his sermons, in a style which is not the less vigorous for being fairly correct. But as a rule his mode of expressing himself is destitute of any pretensions to precision; and in many instances it is a perfect marvel of literary slipshod. Nor is there any ground for believing that the slovenliness was invariably intentional. Sterne's truly hideous French—French at which even the average English tourist would stand aghast—is in itself sufficient evidence of a natural insensibility to grammatical accuracy. Here there can be no suspicion of designed defiance of rules; and more than one solecism of rather a serious kind in his use of English words and phrases affords confirmatory testimony to the same point. His punctuation is fearful and wonderful, even for an age in which the rationale of punctuation was more imperfectly understood than it is at present; and this, though an apparently slight matter, is not without value as an indication of ways of thought. But if we can hardly describe Sterne's style as being in the literary sense a style at all, it has a very distinct colloquial character of its own, and as such it is nearly as much deserving of praise as from the literary point of view it is open to exception. Chaotic as it is in the syntactical sense, it is a perfectly clear vehicle for the conveyance of thought. We are as rarely at a loss for the meaning of one of Sterne's sentences, as we are, for very different reasons, for the meaning of one of Macaulay's. And his language is so full of life and colour, his tone so animated and vivacious, that we forget we are reading and not listening, and we are as little disposed to be exacting in respect to form as though we were listeners in actual fact. Sterne's manner, in short, may be that of a bad and careless writer, but it is the manner of a first-rate talker; and this of course enhances rather than detracts from the unwearying charm of his wit and humour.

It is by the latter of these qualities—though he had the former in almost equal abundance—that he lives. No doubt he valued himself no less, perhaps even more highly, on his sentiment, and was prouder of his acute sensibility to the sorrows of mankind, than of his keen eye for their absurdities, and his genially satiric appreciation of their foibles. But posterity has not confirmed Sterne's judgment of himself. His passages of pathos, sometimes genuine and deeply moving, too often on the other hand only impress the modern reader with their artificial and overstrained sentimentalism. The affecting too often degenerates into the affected. To trace the causes of this degeneration would be a work involving too complex a process of analysis to be undertaken in this place. But the sum of the whole matter seems to be that the "sentiment" on which Sterne so prided himself—the acute sensibilities which he regarded with such extraordinary complacency—were in reality the weakness and not the strength of his pathetic style. When Sterne the artist is uppermost, when he is surveying the characters with that penetrating eye of his, and above all when he is allowing his subtle and tender humour to play around them unrestrained, he can touch the cords of compassionate emotion in us with a potent and unerring hand. But when Sterne the man is uppermost, when he is looking inward and not outward, contemplating his own feelings and not those of his personages, his cunning fails him altogether. In other words he is at his best in pathos when he is most the humourist; or rather, we may almost say, his pathos is never true unless when it is closely interwoven with his humour. (1916)

The more the studied eloquence of Traill condemns, the more I begin to admire Sterne's idiosyncratic style. The more I read Chesterfield, the more I am alienated by the lofty rhetoric of a privileged aristocracy. In reality, effective writing must steer a course between nature and art, between thought and feeling, between spontaneity and logical structure. In this regard, Simon Avery has argued that 'English can still be elegant, sophisticated and subtle when it is immediate and accessible [...] As we emphasize throughout this book, you should always aim for a style which is suitable both for your audience and the context in which your are writing. (Stott and Avery, 2001, 43-66)

Sometimes in writing we are seeking to achieve smooth transitions, pattern, balance, and a rhythmic and melodious sequence; at other times, we need something altogether more jerky and jagged. As we noted above, the use of transition words is highly effective in logical thinking, but one should be warned not to supply too much sign-posting of direction.

In fact, the oppositional quality of nature and art might also be challenged to the extent that the two concepts are radically intertwined. Poetry often captures well this grey area between opposed ideas. Remember that it was Alexander Pope (1688-1744) who famously declared in his 'Essay on Criticism':

Learn hence for ancient rules a just esteem;
To copy Nature is to copy them.

I suspect that nature and classical rules cannot be collapsed into each other. Nonetheless, there appears to be a healthy and necessary tension between them in the process of composition. The crucial point to recall is that careful reflection on an appropriate tone and on the target reader or listener will help the writer to make more informed choices at each stage in the process of composition.

1.6 Power, Rhetoric and Repetition

In addition to the transition words and connectives outlined above we should not forget that the craft of writing is a branch of *rhetoric*: the art of *persuasive* speech. As a cultural practice, rhetoric is clearly a learned activity. It is purposeful and has a stratagem running through it. Accordingly, the common techniques employed, such as the use of a triple repetition, is frequently favoured by politicians and preachers alike in order to achieve emphasis. We recall, for instance, the hammering rhetoric of New Labour's 'Education, education, education.' Or the words of Julius Caesar, 'I came, I saw, I conquered.' In this case the repetition of pronouns together with an element of alliteration is stronger still if we return to the original Latin text: *Veni, vidi, vici*. More specifically, this form is classed as a rhetorical example of *tricolon* and *hendiatris*. The sentence appeared originally in the work of the classical Latin historians Plutarch and Suetonius. In lives on in modern memory, even if our grasp of antiquity is not less firm.

Another famous speech that deploys *anaphora*, or repetition, was delivered by the British Prime Minister Winston Churchill in British Parliament on 4 June 1940:

We shall not flag or fail. We shall go on to the end. We shall fight in France, we shall fight on the seas and oceans, we shall fight with growing confidence and growing strength in the air, we shall defend our island, whatever the cost may be, we shall fight on the beaches, we shall fight on the landing grounds, we shall fight in the fields and in the streets, we shall fight in the hills. We shall never surrender.

The solid foundation for the repetition is *we shall*, with greater weight falling on the variation 'we shall fight.' Subtle variations of the syntactic units provide a sense of strength and supple adaptability. The effect of the speech is simultaneously to portray an emphatic sense of the darkest hour of the war, with defeat and invasion very likely, alongside a vivid presentation of Britain's finest hour of bravery and resistance. Also, this refusal to surrender and this emphatic determination to fight in open combat is contrasted with what Winston Churchill termed the enemy's 'originality of malice, the ingenuity of aggression, which our enemy displays, we may certainly prepare ourselves for every kind of novel stratagem and every kind of brutal and treacherous manœuvre.' The speech therefore employs both the simplicity of repetition as well as the complexity of contrast.

Repetition serves as both a memory device for the speaker and as a way of strengthening an argument in the mind of the listener. As a result there are typically elements of manipulation and facilitation at work in such writings. In the following example the romantic writer William Hazlitt (1778-1830) deployed the repetition of 'They' in order to link the succession of ideas:

On the contrary, we sometimes meet with persons who regularly heat themselves in an argument, and get out of humour on every occasion, and make themselves obnoxious to a whole company about nothing. This is not because they are ill-tempered, but because they are in earnest. Good-nature is a hypocrite: it tries to pass off its love of its own ease and indifference to everything else for a particular softness and mildness of disposition. All people get in a passion, and lose their temper, if you offer to strike them, or cheat them of their money, that is, if you interfere with that which they are really interested in. Tread on the heel of one of these good-natured persons, who do not care if the whole world is in flames, and see how he will bear it. If the truth were known the most disagreeable people are the most amiable. They are the only persons who feel an interest in what does not concern them. They have as much regard for others as they have for themselves. They have as many vexations and causes of complaint as there are in the world. They are general righters of wrongs, and redressers of grievances. They not only are annoyed by what they can help, by an act of inhumanity done in the next street, or in a neighbouring country by their own countrymen, they not only do not claim any share in the glory, and hate it the more, the more brilliant the success, —but a piece of injustice done three thousand years ago touches them to the quick. They have an unfortunate attachment to a set of abstract phrases, such as *liberty, truth, justice, humanity, honour,* which are continually abused by knaves, and misunderstood by fools, and they can hardly contain themselves for spleen. They have something to keep them in perpetual hot water. No sooner is one question set at rest than another rises up to perplex them. They wear themselves to the bone in the affairs of other people, to whom they can do no manner of service, to the neglect of their own business and pleasure. They tease themselves to death about the morality of the Turks, or the politics of the French. There are certain words that afflict their ears, and things that lacerate their souls, and remain a plague-spot there forever after. They have a fellow-feeling with all that has been done, said, or thought in the world. They have an interest in all science and in all art. They hate a lie as much as a wrong, for truth is the foundation of all justice. Truth is the first thing in their thoughts, then mankind, then their country, last themselves. They love excellence, and bow to fame, which is the shadow of it. Above all, they are anxious to see justice done to the dead, as the best encouragement to the living, and the lasting inheritance of future generations. They do not like to see a great principle undermined, or the fall of a great man. They would sooner forgive a blow in the face than a wanton attack on acknowledged reputation. The contempt in which the French hold Shakespeare is a serious evil to them; nor do they think the matter mended, when they hear an Englishman, who would be thought a profound one, say that Voltaire was a man without wit. They are vexed to see genius playing at Tom Fool, and honesty turned bawd. It gives them a cutting sensation to see a number of things which, as they are unpleasant to see, we shall not here repeat. In short, they have a passion for truth; they feel the same attachment to the idea of what is right, that a knave does to his interest, or that a good-natured man does to his ease; and they have as many sources of uneasiness as there are actual or supposed deviations from this standard in the sum of things, or as there is a possibility of folly and mischief in the world. ('Essay On Good Nature', 1816)

The connectives 'On the contrary', 'In short', 'No sooner', 'This', and 'All' are vastly outnumbered by 'They.' Nowadays, it is less certain that we would welcome in this fashion and to this degree the breathless accumulation of the plural pronoun. In this case, the social life of the sentence is becoming a dead uniformity. In cases where attention is drawn too much to the generation of literary effects we tend to draw back from the artifice; we are less willing to submit to the ripple and waves of rhetorical repetition. This writing is a literary *tour de force*, but there is also perhaps the sense that it is a historical curiosity, a museum piece. But such judgments ultimately rely on a question of taste, and as we have noted these factors vary across time and between cultures. The dominant mode of much twentieth-century and contemporary writing is fragmentary and informal. Nowadays, the use of rhetorical flourish, whether it is awkward and stilted, humorous or tragic, is reserved chiefly for politicians, preachers, and for weddings and funerals.

Sometimes repetition may be used effectively in order to present simultaneous but opposed states. In his novel *A Tale of Two Cities* (1859), Charles Dickens (1812-1870) painted alternative pictures of the period of bloody conflict following the French Revolution (1789):

> It was the best of times, it was the worst of times, it was the age of wisdom, it was the age of foolishness, it was the epoch of belief, it was the epoch of incredulity, it was the season of Light, it was the season of Darkness, it was the spring of hope, it was the winter of despair, we had everything before us, we had nothing before us, we were all going direct to Heaven, we were all going direct the other way...

The paired oppositions effectively highlight the mixed emotions, multiple interpretations and conflicted sentiments running through this period. Toward the end of the novel, Chapter 15 offers multiple pictures based on the repetition of 'I see.' But the note is tragic pathos rather than a rousing anthem. The final musical note of the novel is delivered 'with a tender and a faltering voice'; it is spiritual, soft, and ultimately sacrificial, as we recall the famous lines: 'It is a far, far better thing that I do, than I have ever done; it is a far, far better rest that I go to than I have ever known.' The emotional power has the capacity to be lyrical, more beautiful that sublime.

In William Wordsworth's famous poem, 'Lines Written a Few Miles Above Tintern Abbey', the soft 'f' sounds build gently toward the reminiscence and recovery of an intercourse with Nature understood as a potential for regeneration of the soul.

> Five years have passed;
> Five summers, with the length of
> Five long winters! and again I hear these waters...

The repetition links history and personal memory with the natural cycle of the tears and the seasons. With the use of a heightened awareness and the evidence of a reflective sensibility in process, there is a licence granted to formal rhetorical techniques even in the work of the most revered romantic-period poets.

Today, our ears are still potentially open to rousing rhetoric and the emotional pulse of effective speeches. It would be naïve to think otherwise. It is hardly surprising that one of the most famous speeches in modern times was that delivered by Martin Luther King on 28 August 1963. This much admired speech still resonates for us today because of its noble combination of sound and sense working together as ethical indignation and spiritual hope. Again, a key characteristic of this speech was its use of *anaphora*, the repetition of a phrase at the start of sentences. In fact, this rhetorical tool is used throughout the speech. This technique is also used in order to rouse the audience and it serves dramatically as a radical call for action. For example, 'Now is the time' is repeated four times in the sixth paragraph. Similarly the aspirational, evangelical use of the phrase 'I have a dream...' is repeated eight times. Sometimes this phrases opens, and sometimes is closes a group of sentences. Other examples of anaphoric repetition are 'We can never be satisfied'; 'With this faith,' 'Let freedom ring,' and 'free at last.' The genius of the speech, and its significance for the human rights movement, led to the award of a Nobel Peace Prize to Dr King. The speaker was both a politician and a preacher, and although elements of the speech have a rhetorical and rehearsed feel, there is also a strong sense of confident improvisation and audience interaction. Therein lies the power of transformation, achieved by connecting the speaker with his listeners.

For William Sullivan, the head of the Domestic Intelligence Division, the explosive rhetoric was considered as a threat to the stability of the nation. Writing a memo on 30 August 1963 he commented,

> Personally, I believe in the light of King's powerful demagogic speech yesterday he stands head and shoulders over all other Negro leaders put together when it comes to influencing great masses of Negroes. We must mark him now, if we have not done so before, as the most dangerous Negro of the future in this Nation from the standpoint of communism, the Negro and national security.

What all of this illustrates is that the way we choose to start sentences may connect people in such a way that it has a remarkable force and a marvelous power to affect people, and to effect the transformation of society. It is a reminder to pay attention to our choice of words and phrases when we start a sentence, and when we begin to lift our minds to the art of combination, social harmony and political unity.

1.7 The Philosophy of Association

In the philosophy mind and in the psychology of memory the various principles of association are commonly understood in terms of contiguity, similarity and contrast. The sociability and inner connectedness of this process was attended to with keen interest by thinkers, especially in the eighteenth century. In the first place we may locate this feature of human thought in the philosophy of John Locke (1632-1704) which was influential in noting the significance of the association of ideas. In Locke's empirical philosophy it was necessary to link the sensation to the word that describes it, and to be able to distinguish between false connections and compounds that exist in the mind, but not in nature. Furthermore, his knowledge architecture outlined a process of systematic reading. In this there is a discipline with a strong emphasis placed on the notion of connection:

> But the next step towards the improvement of his understanding, must be, to observe the connexion of these ideas in the propositions, which those books hold forth, and

pretend to teach as truths; which till a man can judge, whether they be truths or no, his understanding is but little improved; and he doth but think and talk after the books that he hath read, without having any knowledge thereby. And thus men of much reading are greatly learned, but may be little knowing.

The third and last step therefore, in improving the understanding, is to find out upon what foundation any proposition advanced bottoms; and to observe the connexion of the intermediate ideas, by which it is joined to that foundation, upon which it is erected, or that principle, from which it is derived. This, in short, is right reasoning; and by this way alone true knowledge is to be got by reading and studying.

Building on the work of John Locke, the Scottish philosopher William Hamilton (1788-1856) explored the logic of mental association in terms of *simultaneity* and *affinity* in his *Lectures on Metaphysics* (volume 2, 1860). Additionally, in the case of *redintegration* he expounded a theory based on direct remembrance or reminiscence. These qualities are manifestly essential if we are trying to follow the oral delivery of a speech. In the case of reading a printed text we are afforded the opportunity to look back and re-read earlier sentences if we lose our way, or if we suffer a momentary lapse of concentration. In speech, the use of words signifying connection and transition, or words that deploy rhetorical repetition, help us to focus our attention. They are signpost and memory prompts to stop our minds wandering off.

Earlier still than Locke in the field of literary and philosophical or psychological enquiry, we can identify the significance of the mercurial, playful, shifting imagination of Michel de Montaigne (1533-1592) at work in his brilliant essays on miscellaneous subjects. In one sense we might want to argue that the fluidity of thought as self-expression is a most significant aspect of what we have come think of as the emergence of modern consciousness. In writing about the multiple connections in Montaigne's life that led him to start writing, Sarah Bakewell has noted how is experiences 'made him try a new kind of writing, barely attempted by other writers: that of re-creating a sequence of sensations as they are felt from the inside, following them from instant to instant.' (2011: 23) His style is meandering and sometimes anecdotal, often intertextual, but it is also at times highly personal in a way that commends him as the first memoirist blogger, and as a most significant precursor to the modern world. For the sense of the moment in motion we might also attend to the emergence of the novel in the eighteenth-century, and particularly to the work of Laurence Sterne in his novel *The Life and Opinions of Tristram Shandy, Gentleman* discussed earlier in this introduction. Montaigne, like Sterne, is the great master of flow and process, rather than system and method. As he states in his essay 'Of Repentance':

> I cannot keep my subject still. It goes along befuddled and staggering, with a natural drunkenness. I take it in this condition, just as it is at the moment I give my attention to it. I do not portray being: I portray passing...

Does this fluid, modern notion of consciousness that was emergent in the eighteenth century mean that we are moving, or have transition beyond the formal requirement of rhetorical connectivity?

1.8 Beyond the Logic of Connection

One way of thinking strictly about transition words is that they are to writing what addition, subtraction, multiplication, and division are to mathematics. Or perhaps, equally narrowly, they approximate to the logical operators employed in philosophical discourse. In Chapter 4 of *The Elements of Law Natural and Politic* (1640), for instance, Thomas Hobbes (1588-1679) outlined the concept of *discursion* which is contrasted to the operation of mere dreams:

> Of the Several Kinds of Discursion of the Mind.
>
> THE Succession of conceptions in the mind, Series or Consequence of one after another, may be *casual* and incoherent, as in Dreams for the most part; and it may be *orderly*, as when the former thought introduceth the latter; and this is *Discourse* of the Mind. But because the word Discourse is commonly taken for the coherence and consequence of Words, I will, to avoid equivocation, call it *Discursion*.
>
> 2. The cause of the *Coherence* or Consequence of one

conception to another, is their first coherence or consequence at that time when they are produced by Sense.

Yet, as we have been suggesting, one of the features of modernist literature (perhaps amplifying Laurence Sterne's radical and romantic experiments) was to challenge the enforced, punctuated, structured coherence of literary language. James Joyce (1882-1941) was one of the most celebrated innovators in this regard. The following sample is taken from the final section of *Ulysses* (1922):

> and the sailors playing all birds fly and I say stoop and washing up dishes they called it on the pier and the sentry in front of the governors house with the thing round his white helmet poor devil half roasted and the Spanish girls laughing in their shawls and their tall combs and the auctions in the morning the Greeks and the Jews and the Arabs and the devil knows who else from all the ends of Europe and Duke street and the fowl market all clucking outside Larby Sharans and the poor donkeys slipping half asleep and the vague fellows in the cloaks asleep in the shade on the steps and the big wheels of the carts of the bulls and the old castle thousands of years old yes and those handsome Moors all in white and turbans like kings asking you to sit down in their little bit of a shop and Ronda with the old windows of the posadas glancing eyes a lattice hid for her lover to kiss the iron and the wineshops half open at night and the castanets and the night we missed the boat at Algeciras the watchman going about serene with his lamp and O that awful deepdown torrent O and the sea the sea crimson sometimes like fire and the glorious sunsets and the figtrees in the Alameda gardens yes and all the queer little streets and pink and blue and yellow houses and the rosegardens and the jessamine and geraniums and cactuses and Gibraltar as a girl where I was a Flower of the mountain yes when I put the rose in my hair like the Andalusian girls used or shall I wear a red yes and how he kissed me under the Moorish wall and I thought well as well him as another and then I asked him with my eyes to ask again yes and then he asked me would I yes to say yes my mountain flower and first I put my arms around him yes and drew him down Jo me so he could feel my breasts all perfume yes and his heart was going like mad and yes I said yes I will Yes.

The night-time interior monologue of Molly Bloom presents the raw flow of the thoughts and the captures meticulously the erotic and emotional nature of her preoccupations. This is, of course, an imagined transcription and reconstruction of what's happening inside the mind of an imagined character (ironically based on Homer's Penelope). The text works brilliantly on its own terms and with respect to the requirements of Joyce's idiosyncratic technique. The sense flows in many directions, but it still maintains a focus and purposefulness that readers hang on to, as much as they allow themselves to be carried along the stream of words. The primary recurring transition is 'and' – and while there is a lack of the more intrusive connective words, the sense of underlying sentence units or fragments is not altogether lost. In fact, what makes Joyce's text so powerful in this example is the ghostly presence of the weight, the undertow, coming into dynamic conflict with the ecstatic, orgasmic, free-flow of the expression. The hint of holding back helps to increase the impact of the breakthrough.

Yet another way to interrogate the rhetoric of connection is to challenge the underlying notion of great men making great speeches. Or, perhaps, to challenge the adversarial techniques employed in traditional politics and in the courts of law. Or, to question the predominant role of men in traditional religious rituals. Each of these examples perhaps relies too heavily on the egotistical sublime of the speaker; it relies too heavily on the combative nature of rhetorical debate. In place of these male domains one might consider the new emphasis in the eighteenth century on a more sentimental or feminine discourse. In this regard, the art of connection is based increasingly on the revaluation of the arts of conversation and dialogue. This process implies mutual respect and moderation, and privileges listening as well as speaking skills. Accordingly, as more women moved from the private to the public world, one may discern a depreciation of the classical model of rhetorical delivery. Given that women were not afforded a classical education it seems reasonable to assume that the domestication of discourse contributed significantly to the construction of new forms of public space during the enlightenment. With more women reading and writing the opportunity was created for new forms and styles to emerge and to progressively modify the dominant culture. While this explanation runs the risk of gender polarisation, the exploration of the connection between body and discourse has become a major area of academic research and creative practice.

1.9 *Écriture féminine*

Is the obsession with logic and rationality a limitation imposed on the free flow of writing by the male sex? Is it possible to interrogate order and structure in writing as a masculinised project of control? To think of it as a phallocentric, a logocentric project? On first inspection, it is an odd notion that writing is the product of the shape of our bodies. Yet the anatomical difference between the female and the male body has been considered a sufficient criterion throughout most of recorded time - and across the majority of societies - to constitute a major difference between the sexes. It is a short step from the recognition of difference to the creation of a system of unequal treatment and discrimination.

The idea that writing as a cultural production participates in this power-regime, perhaps even perpetuates it, is clearly not far-fetched. This critical feminist approach claims that the body is written into our daily discourse. Indeed, the project of feminism has not been merely to challenge social, cultural and economic inequality, but to interrogate the complicity of language at all levels in this process of the *construction* of differences. But is it the case that women's writing is *essentially* or *necessarily* different from men's? Is it more accurate to attribute stylistic, technical or structural differences to social opportunities, educational experiences and unchallenged cultural conventions? To return to our earlier examples, are Sterne, Joyce, and Montaigne writing more like women than men? Perhaps we need to attend more to the work of relatively neglected modernist female writers such as Virginia Woolf in order to better understand how writing can flow and connect is a way that is closer to nature than to the artificialities of rational or logical discourse.

In a highly general way, these superimposed binary oppositions have been expressed as a conflict between men and women, nature and art, or between what we are essentially and what is merely a product of social construction. The idea that there is a marked difference between the writing styles and practices of the two sexes has been a contested topic in the academic field since the surge in feminist scholarship of the 1970s. In this regard *Écriture féminine* has emerged as the key term that celebrates and explores the qualities at work in women's writing which are produced by the female body and by female difference. Writers such as Hélène Cixous, Monique Wittig, Luce Irigaray, Chantal Chawaf and Julia Kristeva have been influential in the interrogation of language as a male domain, and in offering a creative and critical challenge to the dominant discourse. Admittedly, the work of post-structuralist feminism has taken many different directions, with different results, and continuing controversy about its use and effectiveness for the emancipation of women. The starting point has been the assertion that women's sexual pleasure has been denied; that deployment of language by men is oppressive; that *jouissance*, play, metamorphic mobility and transgression should be adopted as techniques and strategies for liberation from the patriarchal order. While the slogans and rhetoric are often exhilarating, and the refusal of logic, order and reason is enigmatic and engaging, it does not seem unfair to ask whether the project has enhanced the quality of women's lives, or brought about a revolution of consciousness.

In order to form an opinion of *écriture féminine* the reader is advised to sample some of the key texts by the writers listed above. Some readers will be inspired by the approach taken, while others will be frustrated and alienated by this species of writing. Similarly, the refusal to adopt a clear plan, and a linear structure may also be observed in post-Freudian and post-structuralist works that adopt a 'schizoid' approach. This is a kind of anti-methodology, with planes and zones, and a nomadic tendency, rather than strict linear and logical progression. In *Thousand Plateaux*, for instance, Gilles Deleuze and psychoanalyst Félix Guattari explored this approach. It is the second volume of *Capitalism and Schizophrenia*, and the successor to *Anti-Oedipus* (1972). The aim was to challenge the phallogocentric project. These works may be regarded as courageous experiments or they may be judged to be flawed and failed enterprises. Yet their interest and influence persists, and the deconstuctive revolution is still underway in the academy and beyond.

One further criticism is that *écriture féminine*, like post-structuralism, has failed to live up to its ideals and that it has become a high-level theoretical game with limited impact on women's lives and real world practical issues. Whether as a product of market forces, cultural resistance, or inherent weakness, modernist and postmodern writing has failed to activate a major shift in mainstream creative production. Traditional forms of writing practice are therefore still predominant in the sphere of industry, entertainment, and institutional education. Moreover, there appears also to be a potential discrepancy or difference between the joy of *writing* such works, and the difficulty of *reading* them. This observation returns us to a critique of reading as consumption, but perhaps it also returns us to the desire for transparency in communication, rather than a dream-like, impenetrable opacity. As the previous sentence suggests a recognition of the inevitability of analysis falling back on a linguistic structure derived from the male body and masculine domination alerts us to the notion that the playful inner connections and coherence of *écriture féminine* appear to resist intrusive analysis derived from the exterior.

Nonetheless, the sceptical reaction to *écriture féminine* ought to be qualified by a recognition that in crucial respects contemporary writing and reading practice is shifting away from the traditional forms and modes. On one level, the tyranny of institutional moderation and commercial approval has been disrupted by the ability to express oneself by self-publishing. Nowadays, one can easily participate digitally as a commentator and critic in both the 'high' official or the 'low' transgressive forums; with the result that the sharp cultural hierarchies of the past are being broken down. Writing is increasingly a dialogue, a conversation, and a flow, rather than a top-down imposition. Furthermore, the nature of writing is increasingly fragmentary and ephemeral rather than structured and pre-determined in advance. For conservative critics this new age of writing has produced a dumbing-down of discourse and a free-for-all of unpleasant and rude amateurism. On the other hand, the reading process is also less linear; it is more libertarian and interactive. Increasingly, reading is a mobile and shifting process, whimsical, diversified, aleatory and unlocked from the confines of the sentence, paragraph, the page and the essay. Reading like a butterfly means zigzagging between associated ideas, or wandering aimlessly into unfamiliar and unexpected zones.

Yet all of this is manipulated at another level, since the prescription and anticipation of our existing taste preferences and local milieu are being observed and guided. Also we are reduced to the parameters of the data collected and arranged to suit the needs of increased consumption of the corporate product. The social life of the link is also the guided tour of corporate manipulation and marketing metrics. We are, curiously, already bound into the category of connectivity, whatever our aspirations to liberty and free-will.

1.10 The genesis of this book

To summarise, this is a book about openings and it is a book about transitions. The concept had its inception in a list of connectives which are commonly used in composition. Initially it was to be a modest project; rather like the guides to standard opening moves in chess. But the English language resists the narrow rules of a game. In time, the project became a journey through the writings of many celebrated thinkers and writers who have excelled in the arts, the sciences and the social sciences. The range of sources covered writing that ranged from the practical and the applied, to fiction and to theoretical or philosophical texts. The short guide book became a larger compendium of opening words and connective words. But this research led me to think more deeply about flow and connection in composition. This work then asked for a new opening, and here I was writing an extended introduction that began to displace the original project. And that introduction, which was grounded in linguistics and child development, seemed, in turn, to demand recognition for other openings. In the moment of organized composition I was caught in a vague recognition of a whirlwind of deconstruction over the horizon.

We take the simplicity of connection for granted. Chains of connections, like cause and effect are far more complex than they first appear. I am reminded of the finger on the trigger. The first shot is not the bullet or the gun but the finger on the trigger. (See Jacques Derrida's discussion of the meanings of *Le Declenchement* in *Dissemination*). My project was trapped, either within an immense significance, or within a glorious frivolity. Did it really matter that the most famous narratives begin with a formula? *In the beginning*. Or that in *Grammars of Creation* George Steiner commenced his thoughtful speculations by reminding us 'We have no more beginnings. Incipit; that proud Latin word which signals the start survives in our dusty 'inception'. (2002: 1). The impulse to deploy opening gambits seemed to be both a product of literacy and rhetoric, as well as crucial reminder of an essential underlying orality, presented as the *Once Upon a Time* of the immemorial fairy and folk-tale. After that I was not sure what it was that I had created, discovered, or perhaps just uncovered. The whole seemed to be more than the sum of its parts, and it needed a new beginning. Therefore I am back again, ironically searching for the source code, the beginning of writing, searching for underlying connections in the roots of language and folded into the origin of structured thought and guided emotion.

This was not a story of verbs – the doing of things; or adjectives – the describing of things; or adverbs – the describing of verbs; rather, my topic was the connective tissue of language; the common vocabulary that helps us to join thoughts; it was a defence against isolated moments and risky fragmentation. But the book was also an opening and an ending, looking back at the sentence that came before, and the one that comes after: nonetheless, moreover, accordingly, in the first place...

In a deep sense, perhaps there lies in the grammar of living an ever-present art of connection. At a foundational level language therefore is fundamental to communication and to fulfillment in life. The capacity to create sequence and structure gives meaning to life. By learning to use the micro-system of connection, by reaching outwards from the most common opening and connecting words, we will build bridges of connection within the process of individual creative thought. We will also be connecting with other people, following them more closely. And by the same token, those people who encounter us will be attending to us; they will be in the flow of our thoughts and they will be sharing in our creativity. Therefore this book returns to the basic building blocks of words. In particular, this book proposes that connective and opening words are crucial if we want to secure a foundation for future development that will be a critical and creative force in the world. Connectives link word to world.

Just as we link word to word, we need to connect the sounds to the significances. In language this happens through alliteration, repetition, puns (plays on word) and rhymes. But we must awaken our consciousness to the poetry of life that is there in the words of the world. A sentence should not always draw attention to itself; it has a social life in the flow of the work. There is a risk when a phrase makes a spectacle of itself. When the most suitable words are at our fingertips we have the tools for the job. Clarity in self-expression is the core of confidence and accomplishment. Facility with language can be a powerful force against the alienation, loss and disengagement that restricts and represses human development. That is not to say one cannot be an outsider or a rebel, or that a period of alienation is harmful. But the eloquence of finding solutions and sharing ideas, whether they are radical, revolutionary, or minority, is one of the joys of a connected life that embraces the opening; that folds us into life, and folds life into us. This process is accomplished by means of language.

For any sentence, as for any story, there are so many openings, so many connections. And we are often searching for a smooth transition, the vital or conventional link between one thought and the next. The composition of sentences involves more than the self-contained unit of sense. We also want meaning to flow without obstruction. But often when we try to write there is the pressing sense of so many texts already written. Other openings, other connections. In this regard, in his Preface to his novel *Roderick Hudson* Henry James (1843-1916) questioned 'Where, for the complete expression of one's subject, does a particular relation stop – giving way to some other not concerned in that expression?' Familiarity with language, with literary style and with the experience of reading literature opens up some possibilities, but it also closes down others. We seek to produce meaning by generating our own flow, but we are also in collaboration with the subtle or half-remembered textualities which are already shaping the swerving lines of thought.

When we start to write there is so much still before us – in front, facing us, still to do. Connectives words have this double-edged Janus quality; they face backwards and forwards. They owe their life to the tail of the previous sentence, which they supplement and supplant. Yet they are not fully rooted in the sentences to which they are the head. They are the little unnoticed monsters between the sentences. Modest, minute monsters.

Connectives are also sign-posts, but they do not fit inside the standard world of sign-systems because too much or too little meaning occupies their space. Opening words bear the weight but they pass on the load. They are the gift and the burden of all writing. As markers of meaning they must have a certain presence but when they weigh down on the warp and weft of writing it snaps in our face. When they proliferate we inevitably groan. Too many buts. And yet.

This introduction has attempted to briefly outline the role and function of the connective tissue of language. Subsequently, this book provides a themed illustrations of the most common transitional words and phrases used by writers. In each case, examples are offered of usage drawn from published texts drawn from a wide range of sources and periods.

Ian McCormick

2. THE ART OF LOCATION

The sense of location provides a sense of *where* something is in relation to something else. This use is rather like using a preposition or an adverbial phrase. The words associated with this usage are: above, across, adjacent, adjacent to, alongside, amid, among, around, at the side, away, at this point, before, behind, below, beneath, beside, between, beyond, down, from, further, here, here and there, in front of, in the back, in the background, in the center of, in the distance, in the foreground, in the front, in the middle, just outside, near, nearby, next, on the side, opposite to, over, there, to the left, to the right, to the side, under, up, where, wherever.

These words all suggest a sense of *place* or *location* and are therefore very useful for visual description. But the spatial arrange also provides a sense of where we place ideas. Thus, the sense of something being *Above* easily modulates into the sense of significance suggested in *Above all* ...

The words and phrases outline below provide a complete guide to describing the space around the narrator. These range from the direction of sensory awareness to a sense of how close or how far away are the objects of sense. The words selected help us to generate descriptive passages and particularly useful in writing fiction or travel writing.

Examples of the Art of Location

Above

'Above the Kittatinny the soil is principally composed of gravel and clay, and still farther above the Pokono, partakes so much of the clay as to become very cold and unproductive.' (*The Edinburgh Encyclopedia* - Volume 14, 1832)

Across

'Across the road stood a group of natives in big hats and white calico clothes, all a little the worse for the pulque they had drunk.' (D.H. Lawrence, *The Plumed Serpent*, 1926)

Along

'Along the beach were several Indian wigwams, while numerous pretty bark canoes were going and coming, as this is the Indian stopping place.' (Eliza R. Steele, *A Summer Journey in the West*, 1841)

'Along the *quais* the bookstalls seemed to become almost festive, awaiting the weather which would allow the passerby to leaf idly through the dog-eared books [...]' (James Baldwin, *Giovanni's Room*, 1957)

Amid

'Amid all the bitterness that Mexico produced in her spirit, there was still a strange beam of wonder and mystery, almost like hope. A strange darkly-iridescent beam of wonder, of magic.' (D. H. Lawrence, *The Plumed Serpent*, 1926)

Among

'Thick among the tufts of rank stiff growth lay battered canisters and clots and coils of solid excrement.' (James Joyce, *A Portrait of the Artist as a Young Man*, 1916)

Around

'Here and there warm isles of sand gleamed above the shallow tide and about the isles and around the long bank and amid the shallow currents of the beach were lightclad figures, wading and delving.' (James Joyce, *A Portrait of the Artist as a Young Man*, 1916)

At the back

'At the back a confusion of sheds spread into the home-close from out of two or three indistinct yards.' (D. H. Lawrence, *The Rainbow*, 1915)

At the side

'At the side of the chancel was a new idol: a heavy, seated figure of Huitzilopochtli, done in black lava stone. And round him burned twelve red candles.' (D. H. Lawrence, *The Plumed Serpent*, 1926)

At this point

'At this point a ferry is located, but this does not have a cable. A series of long islands extends from this point down to the upper ferry above Hinton [...]' (Frederick Haynes Newell, *Report of progress of the Division of Hydrography...* U.S. Geological Survey, 1896)

Away

'Away down upon the boulevard at the foot of the rock, tiny trees stood in their own pools of shadow, and tiny people went scurrying about in almost ludicrous importance.' (D. H. Lawrence, *Sons and Lovers*, 1913)

Before

Before the castle a garden lies
   With trees and plants.
The player before the castle will play,
And the trees set out to dance away. (*A Book of Songs*, 1852)

Behind

'Gradually the dark bar on the horizon became clear as if the sediment in an old wine-bottle had sunk and left the glass green. Behind it, too, the sky cleared as if the white sediment there had sunk, or as if the arm of a woman couched beneath the horizon had raised a lamp and flat bars of white, green and yellow spread across the sky like the blades of a fan.' (Virginia Woolf, *The Waves*, 1931)

Below

'But when she reached the head of the dark oak there was Celia coming up, and below there was Mr. Brooke, exchanging welcomes and congratulations with Mr. Casaubon.' (George Eliot,

Middlemarch, 1871)

'Below them, in their holes in the sandstone, pigeons preened themselves and cooed softly.' (D. H. Lawrence, *Sons and Lovers*, 1913)

Beneath

'His troubles will perhaps appear miserably sordid, and beneath the attention of lofty persons who can know nothing of debt except on a magnificent scale.' (George Eliot, *Middlemarch*, 1871)

'We are only lightly covered with buttoned cloth; and beneath these pavements are shells, bones and silence.' (Virginia Woolf, *The Waves*, 1931)

'Beneath she had a dress of fine lavender-coloured cloth, trimmed with fur, and her hat was close-fitting, made of fur and of the dull, green-and-gold figured stuff. She was tall and strange, she looked as if she had come out of some new, bizarre picture.' (D. H. Lawrence, *Women in Love*, 1920)

Beside this

'Beside this it is the centre of an extensive coal basin, which crops out in various places in the neighbourhood.' (Eliza R. Steele, *A Summer Journey in the West*, 1841)

Between

'Between the road and the water, is thrown up a lofty and strong embankment, resembling the dikes in Holland, and meant to serve a similar purpose; by means of which, the Mississippi is prevented from overflowing its banks, and the entire flat is preserved from inundation.' (Charles Kitchell Gardner, *The Literary and Scientific Repository, and Critical Review*, Volume 3, 1821)

'Between us, you say, we could build cathedrals, dictate policies, condemn men to death, and administer the affairs of several public offices. The common fund of experience is very deep.' (Virginia Woolf, *The Waves*, 1931)

'Divided between the claims of obligation to the father, and tender attachment to the daughter, his illness was increased by the tortures of his mind, and he once sincerely wished for that death, of which he was in danger, to free him from the dilemma in which his affections had involved him.' (Elizabeth Inchbald, *A Simple Story*, 1791)

'There was a feeling of connection between the rival men, more than ever since they had fought.' (D. H. Lawrence, *Sons and Lovers*, 1913)

Beyond

'Beyond the foot of the Falls the river is like a slipping floor of marble, green with veins of dirty white, made by the scum that was foam.' (Rupert Brooke, *Niagara Falls*)

Close to

'We had passed two small rocky islands to seaward in the first part of the night, and there was another close to a bluff point on the south side of the bay.' (John Rae, *Narrative of an Expedition to the Shores of the Arctic Sea in 1846 and 1847*)

'Close to the castle was a bridge over the Don in the time of Henry II.' (Joseph Hunter, *The History and Topography of the Parish of Hallamshire*, 1819)

Down

'Down, down, down.' (Lewis Carroll, *Alice's Adventures in Wonderland*, 1865)

Farther off

'Farther off was the great colliery that went night and day.' (D. H. Lawrence, *The Rainbow*, 1915)

'Here, for example, we have the use of speech; in another Planet they may speak by signs; farther off they may not speak at all. Here, reasoning is founded on experience; in another place, experience may add very little; farther off, old men may not know more than children. Here, we are tormenting ourselves concerning the future more than the past; in another Planet, they may torment themselves more concerning the past than the future; farther off they may not torment themselves concerning either one or the other, and these last may not perhaps be more unhappy than either of the former.' (By M. de Fontenelle [Bernard Le Bovier], *Conversations on the Plurality of Worlds*, 1767)

From

'From fairest creatures we desire increase,' (William Shakespeare, Sonnet 1)

Further

'You have gone across the court, further and further, drawing finer and finer the thread between us.' (Virginia Woolf, *The Waves*, 1931)

'They walked up the hill, further and further away from the noise.' (D. H. Lawrence, *Women in Love*, 1920)

Here

'Here every herb, every ear of corn, every flower, every tree, proclaims thy goodness!' (Christoph Christian Sturm, *Reflections on the Works of God in Nature and Providence*, Trans. Rev. Adam Clarke, 1833)

'The current was permanent. Here another beautiful change in the circumstances of the general experiment follows.' (Faraday, *Electricity*, 1840)

'Here the water was first observed to have a deep red tinge as if mixed with blood, but on being examined in a glass was found perfectly colourless; the bottom however seems to account for this appearance, being a soft mud composed of a reddish clay without the smallest mixture of sand, and so smooth that it might be laid on as paint.' (James Tuckey, *Narrative of an expedition to explore the river Zaire*, 1816)

Here and there

'Here and there I strayed through the orchard, gathered up the apples with which the grass round the tree roots was thickly strewn; then I employed myself in dividing the ripe from the unripe; I carried them into the house and put them away in the store-room.' (Charlotte Bronte, *Jane Eyre*, 1847)

In front of

'The captain six paces in front of the right of his company; the first lieutenant the same distance in front of the left; the second lieutenant the same distance in front of the centre, dressed by each other; the cornet on the left of the second of the second lieutenant.' (John Holbrook, *Military Tactics*, 1826)

In the background

'In the first glimpse we had of them all, and at the moment of our passing from the dark cold night into the warm light room, this was the way in which they were all employed: Mrs. Gummidge in the background, clapping her hands like a madwoman.' (Charles Dickens, *David Copperfield*, 1850)

'She walked in brightness, but she knew that in the background those shapes of darkness were always spread.' (Thomas Hardy, *Tess of the d'Urbervilles*, 1891)

'I do not mind them—I mind nothing but my grief—and yet I see and know them all; and even in the background, far away, see Minnie looking on, and her eye glancing on her sweetheart, who is near me.' (Charles Dickens, *David Copperfield*, 1850)

In the centre

'In the centre of this fair valley, just where 'bright waters meet,' is the little town of Ottowa.' (Eliza R. Steele, *A Summer Journey in the West*, 1841)

In the distance

'Coketown in the distance was suggestive of itself, though not a brick of it could be seen.' (Charles Dickens, *Hard Times*, 1854)

'Then there was his other self, in the distance, doing things, entering stuff in a ledger, and he watched that far-off him carefully to see he made no mistake.' (D. H. Lawrence, *Sons and Lovers*, 1913)

In the foreground

'In the foreground is a stream of water issuing from a building, and the poet's dog is there seen drinking.' (*Descriptive Synopsis of the Roman Gallery*, 1817)

'In the foreground of the picture, at the moment of my viewing it, was one of the sons of Lord Moncrieff, (a judge of the Sessions) on horseback, quietly exercising a couple of greyhounds.' (Thomas Frognall Dibdin, *A Bibliographical, Antiquarian and Picturesque Tour in the Northern Counties of England and in Scotland*, 1838)

'Throwing these into distance, rose, in the foreground, a head,—a colossal head, inclined towards the iceberg, and resting against it. (Charlotte Bronte, *Jane Eyre*, 1847)

In the middle

'In the middle of the town was a large, open, shapeless space, or market-place, of black trodden earth, surrounded by the same flat material of dwellings, new red-brick becoming grimy, small oblong windows, and oblong doors, repeated endlessly, with just, at one corner, a great and gaudy public house, and somewhere lost on one of the sides of the square, a large window opaque and darkish green, which was the post office.' (D. H. Lawrence, *The Rainbow*, 1915)

Just outside

'Just outside of this, on a little hill, was Tom Brangwen's big, red-brick house.' (D. H. Lawrence, *The Rainbow*, 1915)

Near

'Near one of these stands a windmill, at which the lord's tenants are bound to grind all their corn and malt.' (James Edwin Thorold Rogers, *A History of Agriculture and Prices in England: (1259-1792)*, 1882)

Near at

'Near at hand, a ragged shifting of banana-trees, bare hills with immobile cactus, and to the left, an *hacienda* with peon's square mud boxes of houses.' (D. H. Lawrence, *The Plumed Serpent*, 1926)

Near to

'They entered a large room, so near to the scaffold that the voices of those who stood about it, could be plainly heard: some beseeching the javelin-men to take them out of the crowd: others crying to those behind, to stand back, for they were pressed to death, and suffocating for want of air.' (Charles Dickens, *Barnaby Rudge*, 1841)

Next to

'Next to the sclerenchyma on the inner side is a circle of large cells with thin walls.' (*Journal of the Institute of Jamaica*, Volume 1, 1892)

On the side of

'On the side of the barranca, fronting the works of Santa Rosalia and La Libertad, the enemy had erected two batteries, the one commanding the other, which threw shot into the works of the besieged, from the distance of half musket shot.' (Vicente Pazos Kanki, *Letters on the United provinces of South America*, 1819)

'On the side of the cavity of the tympanum, which is opposite to the opening of the Eustachian tube, is situated the beginning of another passage, leading into numerous cells, contained in the mastoid process of the temporal bone, and therefore termed mastoid cells: these cells are likewise filled with air.' (Francis Henry Egerton Bridgewater, *The Bridgewater Treatises on the Power, Wisdom and Goodness of God as manifested in the Creation*, 1836)

Opposite

'Opposite its front was a long mound or "grave", in which the roots had been preserved since early winter.' (Thomas Hardy, *Tess of the d'Urbervilles*, 1891)

Over

'Over the level country around Peoria good roads are laid out in every direction.' (Eliza R. Steele, *A Summer Journey in the West*, 1841)

There

'There, there, in the machine, in service of the machine, was she free from the clog and degradation of human feeling. There, in the monstrous mechanism that held all matter, living or dead, in its service, did she achieve her consummation and her perfect unison, her immortality.' (D. H. Lawrence, *The Rainbow*, 1915)

Thither

'Thither he followed, as soon as his servants could complete the necessary preparation for the journey, accompanied by a friend, and attended by a number of his people, determined to obtain Emily, or a full revenge on Montoni.' (Ann Radcliffe, *The Mysteries of Udolpho*, 1764)

To the left ... To the right

'To the left the bright green of the willows by the lake-shore. To the right the hills swerved inland, to meet the sheer, fluted sides of dry mountains.' (D. H. Lawrence, *The Plumed Serpent*, 1926)

Under the

'Under the dome of his tiny hat his unshaven face began to smile with pleasure and he was heard to murmur.' (James Joyce, *A Portrait of the Artist as a Young Man*, 1916)

Underneath

'Underneath, a pile of faggots ready; and at the side, a pile of faggots.' (James Joyce, *A Portrait of the Artist as a Young Man*, 1916)

Upon

'Upon the opposite shore of the river and in this vale, at the foot of the ancient bank, stands the pretty town of Joliet, improperly spelt Juliet.' (Eliza R. Steele, *A Summer Journey in the West*, 1841)

Where there is

'Where there is much desire to learn, there of necessity will be much arguing, much writing, man opinions; for opinions in good men is but knowledge in the main.' (John Milton, *Areopagitica*, 1644)

Within

'Within the fluid world of contemporary prose fiction, however, the occasion has a more dynamic significance.' (Terry Castle, *Masquerade and Civilization*, 1986: 117)

3. THE ART OF TIMING

The words selected supply a sense of *when* something is happening, or to communicate the sense of a logical sequence in *time*. The words in this section can also be compared usefully with the words used to express a sense of *sequence*.

The most common examples of words used in relation to the sense of time are: after, afterward, all of a sudden, as soon as, as often, at about, at last, at the present time, at the same time, at this instant, before, currently, during, earlier, ere long, eventually, even while, finally, first, formerly, forthwith, fourth, from time to time, henceforth, immediately, in a moment, in due time, initially, in the first place, in the future, in the meantime, in the past, in time, instantly, last, later, meanwhile, next, now, occasionally, often, once, presently, prior to, quickly, second, shortly, since, sometimes, soon, sooner or later, straightaway, subsequently, suddenly, then, third, to begin with, today, until, until now, up to the present time, when, whenever, without delay.

These words tend to be very helpful in the writing of a reflective diary or journal. They provide essential clarity in the development of a narrative, where the order of events is especially significant. Some of the words indicate simultaneous actions; others indicate shorter or longer interval between events, or the frequency of an event – whether singular or repeated.

Examples of the Art of Timing

After

'After supper, nothing would serve Miss Darnford and Miss Boroughs, but we must have a dance; and Mr. Peters, who plays a good fiddle, urged it forward.' (Samuel Richardson, *Pamela, or Virtue Rewarded*, 1740)

'After considering the historic page, and viewing the living world with anxious solicitude, the most melancholy emotions of sorrowful indignation have depressed my spirits, and I have sighed when obliged to confess, that either nature has made a great difference between man and man, or that the civilization, which has hitherto taken place in the world, has been very partial.' (Mary Wollstonecraft, *A Vindication of the Rights of Woman*)

'After attacking the sacred majesty of kings, I shall scarcely excite surprise, by adding my firm persuasion, that every profession, in which great subordination of rank constitutes its power, is highly injurious to morality.' (Mary Wollstonecraft, *A Vindication of the Rights of Woman*)

After a while

'After a while, finding that nothing more happened, she decided on going into the garden at once;' (Lewis Carroll, *Alice's Adventures in Wonderland*, 1865)

Afterwards

'Immediately afterwards Hogg tells his own speech about being "not sae yelegant but mair original" than Addison.' (George Saintsbury, *Essays in English Literature 1780-1860*)

'Afterwards it is deprived of its ornaments, and appears in a state of death, till spring comes, and gives it (so to speak) a resurrection.' (Christoph Christian Sturm, *Reflections on the Works of God in Nature and Providence*, Trans. Rev. Adam Clarke, 1833)

All of a sudden

'But my lord, all of a sudden, grew gloomy and fretful, and very unkind sometimes to my lady. This afflicted her very much, as I saw, for she never complained, and she used to try so sweetly to oblige him and to bring him into a good humour, that my heart has often ached to see it.' (Ann Radcliffe, *The Mysteries of Udolpho*,

1794)

'All of a sudden, as he lifted, his cousin stood close to his elbow, pausing a moment on the bend of her foot till the obstructing object should have been removed.' (Thomas Hardy, *Jude the Obscure*, 1895)

As

'As she said these words her foot slipped, and in another moment, splash! she was up to her chin in salt water.' (Lewis Carroll, *Alice's Adventures in Wonderland*, 1865)

As often

'As often happened, they had vanished for a year or more, so that one did not know whether they were alive or dead, and then had suddenly been brought forth to incriminate themselves in the usual way.' (George Orwell, *Nineteen Eighty-Four*, 1949)

As often as

'As often as a study is cultivated by narrow minds, they will draw from it narrow conclusions.' (John Stuart Mill, *August Comte and Positivism*, 1865)

As soon as

'Just then old Carlo opened his door, and he came with a flask in his hand; for, as soon as the Signor saw him, he was as tame as could be, and followed him away as naturally as a dog does a butcher with a piece of meat in his basket.' (Ann Radcliffe, *The Mysteries of Udolpho*, 1764)

'As soon as they had signed their names and come away, and the suspense was over, Jude felt relieved.' (Thomas Hardy, *Jude the Obscure*, 1895)

'On Friday, as soon as he had got himself up as he thought Sue would like to see him, and made a hasty tea, he set out, notwithstanding that the evening was wet.' (Thomas Hardy, *Jude the Obscure*, 1895)

At about

'In 1973, it must have been - at any rate, it was at about the time when he and Katharine had parted.' (George Orwell, *Nineteen Eighty-Four*, 1949)

'At about this time, I began to observe that he was getting flushed in the face; as to myself, I felt all face, steeped in wine and smarting.' (Charles Dickens, *Great Expectations*, 1861)

At last

'At last with creeping crooked pace forth came
An old man, with beard as white as snow.' (Edmund Spenser, *The Faerie Queene*, Book 1, Canto 8: 30)

'At last, as he supported himself, because of his gout, on the back of a chair, I took a little more courage; and approaching him, besought him to acquaint me, in what I had offended him?' (Samuel Richardson, *Clarissa Harlowe*, 1748)

At length

'At length the high white steeple of the town met my eyes.' (Mary Shelley, *Frankenstein: or, The modern Prometheus*, 1818)

'At length they came alongside the *Anne*, — the ship in which Mr. Fairfax had taken his passage.' (Elizabeth Whately, *Reverses; or, Memoirs of the Fairfax family*, 1833)

At other times

'At other times, the whole of the natural world suddenly became 'collectible', as if knowledge were conveyed directly, visibly, tangibly by the objects in a cabinet of curiosities.' (Jenny Uglow, *The Lunar Men: the Friends who Made the Future*, 2003, p. xv)

At present

'At present, every observation, every new discovery we make, fills us with astonishment at the power and wisdom of God; and the desire to arrive at that happy abode, where we shall have a more perfect knowledge of God, and his works, continues to be more and more enkindled in our hearts.' (Christoph Christian Sturm, *Reflections on the Works of God in Nature and Providence*, Trans. Rev. Adam Clarke, 1833)

'At present, we may truly be thankful that a reform in this matter has commenced.' (Albert Day, *Methomania: A treatise on Alcoholic Poisoning*, 1867)

'At present however, to her considering mind, it was as if she had ceased merely to circle and to scan the elevation, ceased so vaguely, so quite helplessly to stare and wonder: she had caught herself distinctly in the act of pausing, then in that of lingering, and finally in that of stepping unprecedentedly near.' (Henry James, *The Golden Bowl*, 1904)

'At present I shall content myself with a single observation.' (Edward Gibbon, *The History of The Decline and Fall of the Roman Empire*, 1782)

At the outset

'At the outset, we were met with the question, What has the Mechanics' Association to do with Art?' (*Massachusetts Charitable Mechanic Association*, 1824)

At the present time

'At the present time we have not sufficient room for our medical staff, some of whom live from one to four miles off the hospital premises. If the appropriation for this item be authorized we could house our entire medical staff.' (*Requests for appropriations to be made at the 1917 session of the Legislature as they have been filed with the Legislative Budget Committee*, New York (State) Legislature Budget Committee, 1916)

'At the present time there are forty churches among the Armenians, and twelve hundred and seventy-seven members.' (Rufus Anderson, *Memorial volume of the first fifty years of the American Board of Commissioners for Foreign Missions*, 1861)

At the same time

'At the same time, not knowing to what dangers she was about to expose herself; nor of whom she could obtain shelter; a stranger to the town, and to all its ways; the afternoon far gone: but little money; and no clothes but those she had on!' (Samuel Richardson, *Clarissa Harlowe*, 1748)

At this point

'At this point it will be necessary to inquire more particularly into the exact position which a missionary occupies.' (Rufus Anderson, *Memorial volume of the first fifty years of the American Board of Commissioners for Foreign Missions*, 1861)

Before

'Before I dismiss the uses of architecture, and indeed of the Arts generally, I cannot but dwell for a moment on the amazing effects they have had, on the labour and mechanical skill of our country.' (Henry Dilworth Gilpin, *An annual discourse before the Pennsylvania Academy of the Fine Arts*, 1827)

'Before approaching these problems – which may after all admit only increasingly refined description rather than solution – one must start with the known, the contemporary record.' (Terry Castle, *Masquerade and Civilization*, 1986, p. 6)

'Before we proceed any further, hear me speak.' (William Shakespeare, *Coriolanus*)

'But before proceeding with the history of this strange fable, it will be well to extract the different accounts given of the Priest-King and his realm by early writers; and we shall then be better able to judge of the influence the myth obtained in Europe.' (Sabine Baring-Gould, *Curious Myths of the Middle Ages*, 1868)

'Before proceeding however to speak of the value of a classical education, we will consider for a moment two causes which have contributed to impair its value in the popular estimation.' (Austin Adams, *An Address Delivered before the Erosophian Society*, 1867)

'Before proceeding to examine this drama, we will just note how meagre were the materials upon which the poet had to work, and we shall then be enabled to eliminate all that is original in the play.' (*Dublin University Magazine*, 1865)

Before the

'That which is aboriginal in America still belongs to the way of the world before the Flood, before the mental-spiritual world came into being.' (D. H. Lawrence, *The Plumed Serpent*, 1926)

Currently

'Currently we are at about 40 million beneficiaries. As this chart shows, that number is going to grow dramatically to over 81 million by 2050.' (*U.S. Congressional Record*, 1874)

'Currently we are, without any question, saving patients' lives, even though, I repeat, there is much about cancer that we do not know.' (*U.S. Congress. Child Labor Bill: Hearings*, 1916)

During

'During the whole evening, Mr. Jellyby sat in a corner with his head against the wall as if he were subject to low spirits.' (Charles Dickens, *Bleak House*, 1852)

'A pause succeeded, during which the honest and irrepressible baby made a series of leaps and crows at little Jane, who appeared to me to be the only member of the family (irrespective of servants) with whom it had any decided acquaintance.' (Charles Dickens, *Great Expectations*, 1861)

'During Jude's temporary absence the waiting-maid spoke to Sue.'

(Thomas Hardy, *Jude the Obscure*, 1895)

'During the interval before the issuing of the certificate Sue, in her housekeeping errands, sometimes walked past the office, and furtively glancing in saw affixed to the wall the notice of the purposed clinch to their union.' (Thomas Hardy, *Jude the Obscure*, 1895)

Earlier

'Earlier it could have annoyed me, but now everything was in good hands and swimming right along.' (Mark Twain, *A Connecticut Yankee in King Arthur's Court*, 1889)

'The earlier it was given in the first stage of the disease, the better. When given freely, so as to produce secretion in the liver, kidneys, and skin, a general and equable re-action soon succeeded.' (James Ewell, *The medical companion: or family physician*, 1827)

Ere long

'Ere long, with the servant's aid, I contrived to mount a staircase; my dripping clothes were removed; soon a warm, dry bed received me.' (Charlotte Bronte, *Jane Eyre*, 1847)

Eventually

'The Library of Bishop SIBLETO was bought, after his death, by Cardinal Asconius COLONNA. Eventually, it was added to the great Collection of the Vatican, of which SIBLETO had been for many years the zealous Librarian.' (Edward Edwards, *Free Town Libraries, their Formation, Management, and History...*, 1869)

'Eventually they broke out of the timber in a disorderly column of fours, striving to return to the ford which they had crossed when they had entered the valley.' (Cyrus Townsend Brady, *Indian Fights and Fighters*, 1904)

'Eventually they got into a squabble among themselves and they discharged these officers, but they continued to draw those salaries.' (*Journal of the Senate of the General Assembly of the State Iowa*, 1935)

Even while

'Even while we look back—and forward—on the changes of empires and the overthrow of states, the rise of some upon the ruin of others, and the dread and interminable rotations of the wheel of fortune, we cannot but feel that there are characters inscribed on the hearts of nations which fortune can never wholly erase.' (John McDiarmid, *The Scrapbook*, 1824)

Finally

'Finally, I believe that many lowly organised forms now exist throughout the world, from various causes.' (Darwin, *The Origin of Species*, 1859)

'But finally they lost patience, seeing that their reformatory efforts went for nothing, and threw both friends and strangers overboard.' (Mark Twain, *What is Man? and Other Essays*, 1906)

'So they determined to cross to the other side and held councils to work out a plan by which the passage might be accomplished. Finally they decided that they must construct a raft.' (John Reed Swanton, *Chickasaw Society and Religion*, 1928)

'Finally, it may be useful to my readers to restate what this book does not set out to do.' (Mary Russo, *The Female Grotesque: Risk, Excess and Modernity*, 1994: 14)

First

'First, let us preserve a purity in our thoughts.' (*Elegant Extracts*, 1790)

'Let me, then, engage your fixed attention,
First, To the peculiar importance of the government of the tongue; and,
Secondly, To the principles by which this government is to be acquired and maintained.
First, Let us reflect on the importance of attaining this control.
Consider, *first*, The dignity and excellence of the faculty of speech.' (Robert Smith, *The Friend*, Volume 8, 1835)

Firstly ... secondly ... thirdly

'... Kate shall draw on her first trousers, made by her own hand; and, that she may do so, of all the valuables in aunty's repository she takes nothing beside, first (for I detest your ridiculous and most pedantic neologism of *firstly*)—first, the shilling, for which I have already given a receipt; secondly, two skeins of suitable thread; thirdly, one stout needle, and (as I told you before, if you would please to remember things) one bad pair of scissors.' (Thomas De Quincey, *Last days of Immanuel Kant and other Writings*, 1847)

Formerly

'Formerly, different ranks, different neighborhoods, different trades and professions, lived in what might be called different worlds; at present, to a great degree in the same.' (J. S. Mill *On Liberty*, 1859)

Forthwith

'Forthwith he gave in charge unto his Squire,
That scarlet whore to keepen carefully;
Whiles he himselfe with greedie great desire
Into the Castle entred forcibly.'
(Edmund Spenser, *The Faerie Queene*, Book 1, Canto 8: 29, 1590)

'Forthwith he made the well his objective. In that country wells were not plentiful.' (Oscar Micheaux, *The Homesteader: A Novel*, 1917)

From then on

'From then on we spoke a new language.' (Jenny Uglow, *The Lunar Men: the Friends who Made the Future*, 2003, p. xx)

From this time

'From this time I carefully avoided all conversation that could possibly lead to religious discussion.' (*Museum of Foreign Literature, Science and Art*, 1831)

Henceforth

'Henceforth it will therefore be restricted to an outline of events, and, in each successive presidency, attention will be principally directed to the nature and objects of the Professorships established or enlarged.' (*The North American Review*, 1841)

'Henceforth it will dedicate to its Creator all its thoughts, memories, hopes, feelings, affections. Henceforth it will seek, above all things, not for its own happiness, but for His glory.' (*The Metropolitan*, 1846)

'Henceforth it never for a moment yielded to the efforts of her physicians — physicians, who combined profound knowledge of their profession, with the liberal, warm and tender sensibilities of men.' (Thomas Peabody Grosvenor, *A Sketch of the Life, Last Sickness, and Death of Mrs. Mary Jane Grosvenor*, 1817)

Hitherto ... henceforth

'Hitherto the Western Patriarchate had rested its claim to ecclesiastical dominion on the secular claims of the Empire; henceforth it substituted divine for imperial right. Hitherto the bounds of the Empire constituted its bounds; henceforth it aspired to be supreme over the world.' (Oswald Joseph Reichel, *The See of Rome in the Middle Ages*, 1870)

Immediately

'Immediately after that, the preses shall adjourn the meeting, and the members shall dismiss. Whisky punch, or toddy, shall be the usual drink of the Society. No wine shall be allowed on any account.' (*The Farmer's Magazine* - Volume 9, 1808)

'But, immediately after that time, the affairs of Rome began to attract the attention of Greek historians 1, and the Romans, though very slowly, began to obtain some acquaintance with the language and literature of Greece.' (William Y. Sellar, *Roman Poets of the Augustan Age: Horace and the Elegiac Poets*, 1892)

'And then immediately after that, the ladies in their rooms began to scream, and Mr. Clarke went up-stairs immediately. The rest of us went out to the front door, and went out-of-doors and looked around the house and there was nobody in sight.' (*Proceedings of the American Society for Psychical Research*, 1913)

'Immediately she went over to her friends (she had many friends by that time) and began to talk to them excitedly.' (Rose Cohen, *Out of the Shadow: A Russian Jewish Girlhood on the Lower East Side*, 1918)

In another moment

'In another moment down went Alice after it, never once considering how in the world she was to get out again.' (Lewis Carroll, *Alice's Adventures in Wonderland*, 1865)

In an instant

'In an instant, while she stood before me repeating these words, she fell down on the floor. I had no need to cry out; her voice had sounded through the house and been heard in the street.' (Charles Dickens, *Bleak House*, 1852)

In due time

'Gillingham saw that his rather headstrong friend would not be able to maintain such a position as this; but he said nothing further, and in due time—indeed, in a quarter of an hour—the formal letter of dismissal arrived, the managers having remained behind to write it after Phillotson's withdrawal.' (Thomas Hardy, *Jude the Obscure*, 1895)

'And, whereas, in due time thereafter, and on the 9th day of May, A. D. 1871, Caroline Hawes, the surviving wife, and one of the heirs-at-law of said deceased, by her attorneys, J. C. Bates and W. H. L. Barnes, filed with the Clerk of this Court...' (*Report of the Proceedings and Arguments in the Probate Court, California*, 1872)

Initially

'Initially we imposed rather serious restrictions on the selection, but currently we are eliminating from transfer to the centers only persons who have long histories of narcotic addiction, people who have serious behavior problems and who have shown acute difficulties in adjustment.' (*Statistical Abstract of the United States*, 1922)

In future

'That in future the ballots for Members of the Jockey Club shall be in the New Rooms, Newmarket, on the Tuesday in the First Spring Meeting, and the Tuesday in the Second October Meeting, in each year.' (Robert J. Hunter, *Racing Calendar*, 1816)

'France is to be treated in future and forever upon the footing of the most favored nation. This is the whole question.' (Walter Lowrie, *American State Papers: Documents, Legislative and Executive*, 1858)

Instantly

'I instantly levelled my gun, in the hope that a chance of saving him might offer.' (*The Saturday Magazine*, 1833)

'Instantly the ghost passed once more and was gone.' (Charles Dickens, *Great Expectations*, 1861)

'Sue instantly emerged from her room, which she had but just entered.' (Thomas Hardy, *Jude the Obscure*, 1895)

In the beginning

'In the beginning, had men continued perfect, it had been just that all things should have remained as they began to Adam and Eve.' (John Milton, *Tetrachordon*, 1645)

In the course of

'In the course of the examination, I was forcibly struck with the great anxiety he expressed to see his son Cary...' (*Decisions of the General Court of Virginia*, 1826)

In the first place

'In the first place, I have collected so large a body of facts, and made so many experiments, showing ...' (Darwin, *The Origin of Species*, 1859)

'In the first place, how are we to account for the strange human craving for the pleasure of feeling afraid which is so much involved in our love of ghost stories?' (Virginia Woolf 'The Supernatural in Fiction', 1918)

'In the first place, the arguments which are urged in favour of Elizabeth apply with much greater force to the case of her sister Mary.' (Macaulay, *The Edinburgh Review*, 1828)

In the future

'Far off in the future, we may venture even now to foresee and calculate that end, and ask, "What will be beyond?"' (Frances Power Cobbe, *Broken lights: an inquiry into the present condition and future prospects of faith*, 1864)

'You will see in the future a great blessing in store for your children. You will see that, for the benefit of Africa, no drunkard, idler, or convict ought to be permitted to go there.' (Jacob Dewees, *The Great Future of America and Africa: An Essay Showing Our whole Duty to the Black Man*, 1854)

In the long run

'In the long run the Texans had the best of it, and the Mexicans found the land north of the Rio Grande untenable.' (Walter Prescott Webb, *The Great Plains*, 1931)

'None, in the long run, will suffer but the selfish aristocrats who have hitherto saved themselves from insolvency by levying an enormous tax upon the other classes of the community.' (*Blackwood's Magazine*, 1838)

'In the long run, those who obey become accustomed to the yoke; the sword is drawn, and the factious are hurled to the dust.' (*Literary Gazette*, 1820)

In the past

'Yet now as in the past there is a considerable percentage of those born who cannot accept of education; a low mentality makes them fitted for doing the lower types of labor.' (*The Rotarian*, 1928)

'In the past the annual timber tax was largely offset by an enhanced value of the timber itself. Stumpage values, however, ceased to grow 6 or 7 years ago, they became stationary and recently have tended steadily downward.' (Fred Rogers Fairchild, *Forest Taxation in the United States*, 1935)

'In the past, also, war was one of the main instruments by which human societies were kept in touch with physical reality.' (George Orwell, *Nineteen Eighty-Four*, 1949)

In time

'In time they were visited by a large worm, the bite of which was considered poisonous.' (John Fanning Watson, *Annals of Philadelphia and Pennsylvania, in the Olden Time*, 1857)

'In time they were greatly afflicted with small-pox, and fifty-six of their number now rest among the other dead, beneath the surface of the beautiful Washington Square.' (John Fanning Watson, *Historic Tales of Olden Time*, 1833)

In times

'In times of confusion, every active genius finds the place assigned him by nature: in a general state of war, military merit is the road to glory and to greatness.' (Edward Gibbon, *The History of The Decline and Fall of the Roman Empire*, 1782)

Just then

'Just then she heard something splashing about in the pool a little way off, and she swam nearer to make out what it was: at first she thought it must be a walrus or hippopotamus, but then she remembered how small she was now, and she soon made out that it was only a mouse that had slipped in like herself.' (Lewis Carroll, *Alice's Adventures in Wonderland*, 1865)

'Just then Jesse Roberts said, "Yes; stick it to him;" and deceased said to me, "No you won't; you won't get away from here." '(*The Southwestern Reporter*, 1808)

Last thing

'The last thing one knows in constructing a work is what to put first.' (Blaise Pascal 1623-1662)

Lastly

'Lastly, it is a remarkable fact, as proved by the foregoing quotations, that the same fashions in modifying the shape of the head, in ornamenting the hair, in painting, tattooing, in perforating the nose and lips, or ears, in removing or filling teeth, &c., now prevail, and have long prevailed, in the most distant quarters of the world.' (Charles Darwin, *The Descent of Man*)

Later

'A few days later, and it will be indeed too late.' (Walter Scott, *Ivanhoe*, 1820)

Many a time

'Many a time have you and I sat in our early days upon the banks of the Passaic, watching these brilliant creatures as they starred the black robe of night, but we never beheld them so large, and dazzling as these western lights.' (Eliza R. Steele, *A Summer Journey in the West*, 1841)

Meanwhile

'Meanwhile, in the world outside, people carried on devouring romances, thrillers and historical novels without the faintest idea that the halls of academia were beset by these anxieties.' (Terry Eagleton, *Literary Theory*, 1983: 26)

'Meanwhile, Brown the manservant announces that a strange young man has arrived to breakfast.' (Virginia Woolf, 'Henry James's Ghost Stories' 1921)

'Meanwhile, those things in which you may really excel go for nothing, because they cannot judge of them.' (William Hazlitt, "On the Disadvantages of Intellectual Superiority," 1822)

Next

'William Earl of Pembroke was next, a man of another mould and making, and of another fame and reputation with all men, being the most universally loved and esteemed of any man of that age...' (Edward Hyde (1st Earl of Clarendon), *The History of the Rebellion and civil Wars in England*, 1839)

'Next, shoemaker; I don't know if he was here at election. Next, a man who keeps hotel, he is a Frenchman, I forget his name. Next is Mr. Bivins, farmer; he has two sons, I think, old enough to vote. Next is Mr. Palmer, lumber business [...]' (*Congressional Edition*, 1879)

'Next I think that you may object that in all this I have made too much of the importance of material things.' (Virginia Woolf, *A Room of One's Own*, 1929)

Not yet

'Not yet since his marriage had Maggie so sharply and so

formidably known her old possession of him as a thing divided and contested.' (Henry James, *The Golden Bowl*)

Now

'Now the serious use the habitual stress which the mind lays upon the expectation of a given order of events, following one another with a certain regularity and weight of interest attached to them.' (William Hazlitt, *Lectures on English Comic Writers* p. 6)

'Now is the winter of our discontent / Made glorious summer by this son of York;' (William Shakespeare, *Richard III*)

'Now, fair Hippolyta, our nuptial hour / Draws on apace.' (William Shakespeare, *A Midsummer Night's Dream*)

'Now say, Châtillon, what would France with us.' (William Shakespeare, *King John*)

'Now, as all psychological treatment is useless without the earnest and hopeful assistance of the patient, and as no sympathetic co-operation can be expected from one who has no faith in the ultimate success of his efforts, it follows that the element of hope should be carefully nourished as a powerful stimulant to the other means employed.' (Albert Day, *Methomania: A treatise on Alcoholic Poisoning*, 1867)

Now and then

'Only now and then, in one of the house-windows vegetables or small groceries were displayed for sale.' (D. H. Lawrence, *The Rainbow*, 1915)

Occasionally

'Occasionally our track lay close to the shore, and we gazed into the forest's deep recesses; now a dark jungle is before us, haunt of the wolf and the panther;' (Eliza R. Steele, *A Summer Journey in the West*, 1841)

Often

'Sometimes, too, he brought music of his own, and awakened every fairy echo with the tender accents of his oboe; and often have the tones of Emily's voice drawn sweetness from the waves, over which they trembled.' (Ann Radcliffe, *The Mysteries of Udolpho*, 1794)

'Often, however, I have recourse to stereotypical grotesques.' (Mary Russo, *The Female Grotesque: Risk, Excess and Modernity*, 1994: 14)

Once more

'Once more I return to the early poetry of France, with which our own poetry, in its origins, is indissolubly connected.' (Matthew Arnold, *The Study of Poetry*, 1880)

Once upon a time

'Once upon a time — we like this old school-boy-tale-method of opening a subject; there is something racy in the very smack of it. Once upon a time, a laughter-loving monarch proposed to the philosophers, projectors, wise men, and civil engineers of his court, with a gravity becoming the importance and intricacy of the matter, the following problem: —' (Alexander Gordon, *An historical and practical treatise upon elemental locomotion, by means of Steam Carriages on Common Roads*, 1832)

One day

'One day her Uncle Tom came in out of the broiling sunshine heated from walking.' (D. H. Lawrence, *The Rainbow*, 1915)

Presently

'Presently he knelt down, and with a look so solemn as she had seldom seen him assume, and which was mingled with a certain wild expression, that partook more of horror than of any other character, he prayed silently for a considerable time.' (Ann Radcliffe, *The Mysteries of Udolpho*, 1764)

'Presently she began again.' (Lewis Carroll, *Alice's Adventures in Wonderland*, 1865)

Prior to

'Prior to this, we had no certain information respecting the correct position of any of its various points, or the almost innumerable reefs which bound its shores.' (James Raymond Wellsted, *Travels in Arabia*, 1838)

Quickly

'Quickly she started up, leaped right upwards many times; then ran to and fro with an hundred odd gesticulations. She beat herself on the head, tore her hair, and attempted to run into the fire.' (John Wesley, *The Works of the Rev. John Wesley*, 1829)

'Quickly she learnt to read, quickly she learnt to believe and pray, and give thanks. Most happy were the accounts we received of her during the few months that she survived our departure. She was never lonely, never afraid of being alone [...]' (*The Monthly*

Packet, 1861)

Secondly

'*Secondly*, it may be pretended, that the decline of eloquence is owing to the superior good sense of the moderns, who reject with disdain all those rhetorical tricks employed to seduce the judges, and will admit of nothing but solid argument in any debate or deliberation.' (David Hume, 'Of Eloquence', *Essays*)

Shortly

'Shortly afterwards he was sent in the command of this regiment to Dominica.' (*The Gentleman's Magazine*, 1824)

'Shortly after that period he left Congress, and had no opportunity of making known his sentiments in reference to the protective system, which shortly after began to be agitated.' (*Debates in Congress*, 1833)

'[...] that shortly after that again, the deceased went out to the market ; that shortly after that again, the deceased and the prisoner returned to her house ; that shortly after that again, the prisoner called the deceased [...]' (*Decisions of the Nizamut Adawlut*, India, Volume 3, 1853)

'Shortly afterwards, he was appointed superintendent postmaster of the province, and, whilst in that office, displayed great activity, and placed the post office in an ameliorated condition.' (Henry James Morgan, *Sketches of Celebrated Canadians*, 1862)

Simultaneously

'Simultaneously he has contrived new sources of revenue, as, for example, by means of a reasonable increase of the spirit duties and by his extension of the succession duties to real and personal property. Simultaneously he has, with a daring and resolute hand, we are almost tempted to say, perfected that bold revision of the tariff upon which Sir Robert peel was the first to adventure.' (*The Westminster Review*, Volume 35, 1869)

'Simultaneously he commenced the organisation of the Austrian forces, the establishment of a secret understanding with Prussia, Bavaria, and Saxony, speaking to them all of a peace to be concluded on terms favourable to Germany, and then [...]' (Marie Joseph L. Adolphe Thiers, *History of the Consulate and the Empire of France under Napoleon*, 1857)

Since

'Since the death of her aunt, her mind had acquired new firmness and vigour.' (Mary Shelley, *Frankenstein: or, The modern Prometheus*, 1818)

Sometimes

'Sometimes he stands— sometimes he sits — and, most commonly, does both, several times in the course of a single meeting. Sometimes he tries to conciliate, by assuring the people of his general will — sometimes he states truth — sometimes [...]' (*Missionary Register*, 1828)

'Sometimes he hath bread, and sometimes he is hungry; sometimes he hath clothes, and sometimes is naked; sometimes he hath a house, and sometimes he hath none; sometimes he hath friends, and sometimes he hath none [...]' (*Religious Tract Society*, Volume 11, 1850)

Soon

'Soon her eye fell on a little glass box that was lying under the table: she opened it, and found in it a very small cake, on which the words `EAT ME' were beautifully marked in currants.' (Lewis Carroll, *Alice's Adventures in Wonderland*, 1865)

Sooner or later

'Mrs. Joe was prodigiously busy in getting the house ready for the festivities of the day, and Joe had been put upon the kitchen doorstep to keep him out of the dust-pan,—an article into which his destiny always led him, sooner or later, when my sister was vigorously reaping the floors of her establishment.' (Charles Dickens, *Great Expectations*, 1861)

Straight away

'Straight away she headed towards the south, not turning to one side or the other. The captain was still seen waving his hand as long as he could be discerned ; but so rapidly did the monster tow him along, that he was soon lost to sight in the horizon [...]' (William Henry G. Kingston, *At the South Pole*, 1870)

'He had never seen a dog go mad, nor did he have any reason to fear madness; yet he knew that here was horror, and fled away from it in a panic. Straight away he raced, with Dolly, panting and frothing, one leap behind;' (Jack London, *Call of the Wild*, 1903)

Subsequently

Subsequently delegates did attend, but the synod, declining to become identified with the General Synod, remained independent. (*Religious Bodies: 1916: Separate Denominations, History, Description, and Statistics. Part 2.* United States Bureau of the Census)

Subsequently, and during the remainder of his stay in Paris, he humoured her fancy, and led her to imagine that he had sufficient influence with Cromwell to prevail on him to interest her father on her behalf... (S. C. Hall, *The Buccaneer*, 1840)

Suddenly

'Suddenly she came upon a little three-legged table, all made of solid glass; there was nothing on it except a tiny golden key, and Alice's first thought was that it might belong to one of the doors of the hall; but, alas! either the locks were too large, or the key was too small, but at any rate it would not open any of them.' (Lewis Carroll, *Alice's Adventures in Wonderland*, 1865)

Then

'Then he took up beaten and chiselled metal work.' (D. H. Lawrence, *The Rainbow*, 1915)

'Then I went on, thinking, thinking, thinking; and the fire went on, burning, burning, burning; and the candles went on flickering and guttering, and there were no snuffers—until the young gentleman by and by brought a very dirty pair—for two hours.' (Charles Dickens, *Bleak House*, 1852)

'Then he set-to to make a head of Ursula, in high relief, in the Donatello manner.' (D. H. Lawrence, *The Rainbow*, 1915)

Thirdly

'Thirdly, even if the received opinion be not only true, but the whole truth; unless it is suffered to be, and actually is, vigorously and earnestly contested, it will, by most of those who receive it, be held in the manner of a prejudice, with little comprehension or feeling of its rational grounds.' (J. S. Mill, *On Liberty*, 1859)

To begin with

'To begin with, she is doing a very silly thing. Again, she is doing that which compromises her in the eyes of all sensible young men.' (Josiah Gilbert Holland, *Titcomb's Letters to Young People, Single and Married*, 1858)

'To begin with, she has had no general experience of life to entitle her to speak with authority: to go on with hers is not an example I should wish to imitate.' (Charles Dickens, *All the Year Round*, Volume 4, 1870)

'To begin with, she had a sneaking fondness for Arthur, begotten of old associations.' (*Macmillan's Magazine*, 1872)

Until then

'Until then, there is nothing for them but implicit obedience to an Akbar or a Charlemagne, if they are so fortunate as to find one.' (J. S. Mill, *On Liberty*, 1859)

'May 6th.

Until this time
Until this time the Naturalists were obliged to content themselves with the small animals the towing net afforded them, but they were now gratified by the capture of albicore and bonito, many of both being taken by the grains and hook.' (James Tuckey, *Narrative of an expedition to explore the river Zaire*, 1816)

When

'When a man assumes public trust, he should consider himself as public property.' (Thomas Jefferson)

'When we survey the wretched condition of man under monarchical and hereditary systems of government, dragged from his home by one power, or driven by another, and impoverished by taxes more than by enemies, it becomes evident that those systems are bad, and that a general revolution in the principle and construction of governments is necessary.' (Thomas Paine, *The Rights of Man*, 1791)

'When the mind has once begun to yield to the weakness of superstition, trifles impress it with the force of conviction.' (Ann Radcliffe, *The Mysteries of Udolpho*, 1764)

'When shall we three meet again.' (William Shakespeare, *Macbeth*)

When once

'When once any object has been seen, it is impossible to put the mind back to the same condition it was in before it saw it.' (Thomas Paine, *The Rights of Man*, 1791)

While

'While I sat thus, looking at the fire, and seeing pictures in the red-hot coals, I almost believed that I had never been away; that Mr. and Miss Murdstone were such pictures, and would vanish when the fire got low; and that there was nothing real in all that I remembered, save my mother, Peggotty, and I.' (Charles Dickens, *David Copperfield*, 1850)

Without delay

'After three or four passages, they became small, and the pain began to return. Without delay she began again to take the same doses; there was no operation after she re-commenced, until she had taken four closes, when the same kind of passages came away [...]' (John Eberle, *The American Medical Recorder*, 1824)

'Without delay she then, with her arm still extended, lifts the child out of this hanging position so far upwards that the end of the child's trunk falls gradually by its own weight, whereby the weight of the child now falls on the thumbs [...]' (*Handbook of Midwifery for Midwives*, 1884)

4. THE ART OF COMPARISON

A repertoire of words and phrases is available in order to point to a *comparison* of two ideas. In rational discourse, debate and argument these clusters of words show that the writer is able to establish essential links between thoughts.

This may be achieved by deploying words such as: additionally, again, also, and, as, as a matter of fact, as well as, by the same token, comparatively, correspondingly, coupled with, equally, equally important; furthermore, identically, in addition, in like manner, in the light of, in the same fashion, in the same way, like, likewise, moreover, not only ... but also, not to mention, of course, similarly, to say nothing of, together with, too.

As these examples above demonstrate the ruling idea is *similarity*.

The words used to express a sense of comparison may profitably be opposed to the words listed in the next chapter which outlines the repertoire of words available to express the sense of contrast or differences between ideas.

Examples of the Art of Comparison

Additionally

'Additionally, it had become a resolution, when leaving Lancaster, as my absence would go near to break the hearts of my parents, never to break upon my worthy father's purse.' (John Joseph Henry, *An accurate and interesting account of the hardships and sufferings of that band of heroes who traversed the Wilderness in the Campaign Against Quebec in 1775*, 1812)

'Additionally, it may be noted down here, that tickling and itching, form two kinds of sensual feelings, strictly belonging to bodily feeling.' (Peter Kaufmann, *The Temple of Truth: Or the Science of Ever-progressive Knowledge...*, 1858)

'Additionally it has merit in its cheapness and convenience; it is ever ready, is easily prepared, and simple in its application. Its use renders the surgeon in many instances quite independent of the commercial instrument-maker —' (*Transactions of the American Orthopaedic Association*, 1893)

Again

'Again, there are many substances which contain elements such as would be expected arrange themselves at the opposite poles of the pile, and therefore in that respect fitted for decomposition, which yet do not conduct.' (Michael Faraday, *Electricity*, 1833)

'Others, again there are, that through a pious education, common convictions, knowledge of the truth, and such like, are convinced that their present course of life is sinful and dangerous, but flatter themselves that all shall yet be well;' (James Meikle, *Solitude Sweetened: Or, Miscellaneous Meditations on Various Religious Subjects*, 1818)

'Again, there are hills of marble which will vie with any in the world: and I have seen millstones taken from the quarry not surpassed by the French burr for manufacturing of flour, being the same to all appearance.' (*Prospectus of the Missouri Iron Company*, 1837)

Also

'Also it must be a malicious burning; otherwise it is only a trespass ; and therefore no negligence or mischance amounts to it.'

(William Blackstone, *Commentaries on the laws of England: in four books*, 1836)

'Also, isn't technique capable of good and bad uses?' (Carl Skrade, *God and the Grotesque*, 1974: 50)

'Also it must often happen that various prolixities and redundancies occur in the course of an interchange of letters, which must hang as a dead weight on the progress of the narrative.' (Walter Scott, *Redgauntlet*, 1824)

'Also it must be admitted that with us the pirate spirit dwelt far far down into recent history.' (*Blackwood's Edinburgh Magazine*, Volume 112, 1872)

And

'And by the latter in consequence of the former?' (Coleridge, *Biographia Literaria*, 1817)

'Dying is a very dull, dreary affair. And my advice to you is to have nothing to do with it.' (W. Somerset Maugham)

'And *she* was very happy too. Her young heart's love had been pent up within her own breast for years.' (*Museum of Foreign Literature, Science and Art*, 1831)

As

'As for me, I see no such great cause why I should either be fond to live or fear to die. I have had good experience of this world, and I know what it is to be a subject and what to be a sovereign. Good neighbours I have had, and I have me with bad: and in trust I have found treason.' (Queen Elizabeth I, 1586)

'As civilization advances, poetry almost necessarily declines.' (Macaulay, *Literary Essays*, 1825)

As ... as

'Glasses of such magnifying powers will make a lark appear as big as a fowl, a fowl as big as a full-grown cock turkey, ducks and geese as big as bustards and swans, a leg of mutton as large as a hind quarter of beef, turnips and potatoes of the size of melons [...]' (*The life, adventures, and opinions of Col. George Hanger: Written by himself*... Edited by William Combe, 1801)

'As big as a moderate horse.' (Georges Cuvier, *The Animal Kingdom*, 1827)

'A bird can fly twice as fast as a horse can run. A horse can draw ten times as much as a man. An elephant can draw five times as much as a horse.' (Harvey Prindle Peet, *Elementary Lessons, Being a Course of Instruction*, 1850)

As a matter of fact

'As a matter of fact, the grocers are perfectly aware of the kinds of tea most frequently adulterated, and understand the use of a magnet and hot water as well as we do.' (William Crookes, *The Chemical News and Journal of Physical Sciences*, 1773)

'As a matter of fact it is not uncommon for portions of works of art clearly subject-matter for copyright protection to be adopted and used as trade-marks.' (*Library of Congress Copyright Office*, 1789)

As a rule

'As a rule, he is deficient in vitality (*The Popular Science Monthly*, 1885)

'His dialogue is, as a rule, extraordinarily slipshod and unequal: here there is no fault to find with it.' (George Saintsbury, *Essays in English Literature 1780-1860*)

As usual

'Toad, as usual, comes out on the top!' (Kenneth Grahame, *Wind in the Willows*, 1908)

' "As usual, everything is beautifully indefinite," replied Harry. "However, we may as well strike right in and see what we can do. Shall we go through the house?" ' (*The Bradys and the Conspirators; Or, The Case That Came From Mexico*, 1911)

'And, as usual, he allowed it to get about that he had made a great profit on his cargo.' (Joseph Conrad, *Nostromo*, 1904)

'As usual, the highest mortality from these diseases was in July, August, September, and October.' (*Birth statistics for the birth registration area of the United..., Volume 5.* United States Department of Commerce: Bureau of the Census, 1919)

As well as this

'But at this I can offer no judgment without knowing the matter from that side as well as this, which I should be very glad to do, that I might, if there be occasion, be better able to argue it with them here.' (William Temple, *Works*, 1770)

'And I wonder why, with your eagle's eyes, you did not espy another foul contradiction in his words as well as this, and say, that he supposes a man may walk according to the rule of holy obedience, and yet vitiate his holy faith with a lewd and wicked conversation.' (William Chillingworth, Edward Knott, *The religion of Protestants: a safe way to Salvation*, Volume 2, 1799)

'The prince's manifesto is now sold publickly, and in all languages, as well as this inclosed fine picture ; which infamous liberty they may as well take, as the prince of Orange to speak, in his manifesto, so basely and falsely, of the great belly of the Queen, and of the supposed Prince of Wales.' (James Macpherson, *Original Papers; Containing The Secret History of Great Britain*, Volume 1, 1775)

'Had all the other arts, as well as this, been less the fruits of education and study, than the happy gifts of nature, there is no doubt but there would have existed a perfect equality between men and women.' (Stéphanie Félicité Comtesse de Genlis, *Tales of the Castle: Or, Stories of Instruction and Delight*, 1785)

By the same token

'By the same token he rode safely—the looseness of his bones accommodating itself with singular facility to the irregularities in the pace of the surprised animal beneath him.' (*The New York Mirror*, 1834)

By the same token, I made love to a pretty girl, who was desperately smitten with my handsome face. (*Southern Literary Messenger*, 1840)

'By the same token, I robbed the orchard three times — what of that? It was the old Abbot's residence when there was plague or sickness at Abingdon.' (Walter Scott, *Kenilworth*, 1821)

Comparatively

'Comparatively few birds are brought from England.' (*Farmer's Bulletin*, United States Department of Agriculture, 1903)

And comparatively few as the instances are, still in the case of a custom so strange and unnatural, we are fully entitled to call it a systematic use. (*The Ecclesiologist*, 1850)

'How comparatively barbarous are the line of villas, so much boasted of by travellers, on the Neva, on the road from St. Petersburgh ; or any other villas near the other capitals of Europe!' (*The Lady's Book*, 1830)

Comparatively speaking

'Comparatively speaking, they now read the same things, listen to the same things, see the same things, go to the same places, have their hopes and fears directed to the same objects, have the same rights and liberties, and the same means of asserting them.' (J. S. Mill *On Liberty*, 1859)

Correspondingly

'The reagent employed in these experiments was alizarin, an alcoholic solution of which will readily detect, one part of soda in three millions of water, and a correspondingly small amount of potash, ammonia, &c' (William Crookes, *The Chemical News and Journal of Industrial Science*, 1774)

'Correspondingly, the interest expressed in used cars has declined.' (*University of Michigan. Institute for Social Research*, 1779)

'Correspondingly, most translations will not be easy to read, and there will always be room for debate.' (*The Journal of Ecclesiastical History* 62.3 (2011): 579)

Coupled with

'Desert is a term, in relation to which I have on several occasions observed, that, though it is with propriety coupled with reward, it is not with propriety coupled with punishment: if, however, it be assumed to be properly coupled with punishment, [...]' (Jeremy Bentham, *Lord Brougham Displayed...*, 1832)

'Coupled with this is love of country, its institutions and the purposes of its government.' (*Boys' Life*, July 1917)

Equally

'Equally unsuccessful were the trials made by Ehrenberg with the indigo and gumlac of commerce, which are always contaminated with a certain quantity of white lead, a substance highly deleterious to all animals; but, at length, by employing an indigo which was quite pure, he succeeded perfectly.' (Francis Henry Egerton Bridgewater, *The Bridgewater Treatises on the Power, Wisdom and Goodness of God as manifested in the Creation*, 1836)

Equally important

'Equally important is the provision made by most good colleges today for a faculty advisor or a faculty committee to counsel foreign students -- ' (*The Rotarian*, 1942)

'Equally important is it, that their parents should enlist the consciences of their children, to secure a ready and cheerful obedience.' (*The Religious Monitor*, 1839)

'Equally important is it (and perhaps in some respects even more so) to determine the absence of pregnancy in cases where it has been supposed to exist.' (Edward Rigby, *A System of Midwifery*, 1841)

Furthermore

'... and furthermore, the people do not approbate the course of said party in the affair ; and furthermore, the people of this county desire to live in peace and amity; and furthermore, the parties who acted in this affair have left us immediately, ...' (*Annual Report of the Commissioner of Indian Affairs*, 1860)

'Furthermore, the manure might be, and often is, taken from the heap where diseased plants have been thrown to compost, or it may be from animals that have fed on diseased cabbage.' (*Farmers' Bulletin*, 1869)

'Furthermore the question arises, When will the Constitution of Ninety-three, of 1793, come into action? Considerate heads surmise, in all privacy, that the Constitution of Ninety-three will never come into action.' (Thomas Carlyle, *The French Revolution: A History*, 1838)

'Furthermore, the fine line drawn in literary studies between those works worthy of scholarly attention and inclusion in the canon and those assigned to the category of popular literature if often contingent upon the author's sex and choice of genre.' (Resa L. Dudovitz, *The Myth of Superwoman Women's Bestsellers in France and the United State*, 1990: 20)

Identically

'John yesterday, and John ten years ago, and today, is identically the same person, although the matter of his body has undergone many changes, as well as the dispositions and habits of his mind.' (Isaac Taylor, *Elements of thought: or, concise explanations*, 1853)

'Thus having commenced with telling us that the sacrifice of the Mass, was identically the same as the sacrifice of the cross, we are now to learn that so far from being identically the same, they actually differ on those particulars that more than all else constitute the essence of a sacrifice – [...] And yet they tell us, that they are one and the same – identically the same!' (Michael Hobart Seymour, *Evenings with the Romanists*, 1854)

'The church of to-day is identically the church of yesterday, the church of yesterday is identically the church of the day before, and thus step by step back to the apostles ; on the other hand, the church in the time of the apostles is identically the church of their successors down through all succeeding generations of individuals as us.' (*Catholic World*, Volume 13, 1871)

In addition

'but the poor man is exposed to great hazard; and, in addition, it is to be feared, the conversation which goes on is seldom likely to improve his mind, or increase his loyal obedience to established authority;' (*Monthly Magazine and British Register*, 1819)

'In addition to the facts stated in the return, it was proved to the said Court, that the petitioners are citizens of the United States.' (*Decisions of the General Court of Virginia*, 1826)

'The conditions required to produce germination are, exposure to moisture, and a certain quantity of heat; in addition, it is necessary that a communication with the atmosphere should be provided, if germination is to be maintained in a healthy state.' (John Lindley, *The Theory and Practice of Horticulture*, 1855)

'In addition, it is found that the prostate, or any one of its lobes, may become enlarged; and it has become the universal belief, since the days of Sir E. Home, that stricture in the deeper portions of the canal depends upon this cause, or upon abscess in the neighborhood.' (William Acton, *Practical Treatise on Diseases of the Urinary and Generative Organs in both Sexes*, 1858)

In like manner

'In like manner, any thing we must not think of makes us laugh, by its coming upon us by stealth and unawares, and from the very efforts we make to exclude it.' (William Hazlitt, *Lectures on English Comic Writers*, 1845)

'In like manner, it was rightfully assumed by Caius Caligula, he being the adopted grandson of Tiberius; but he set the first example of departing altogether from the idea that it was a title hereditary in the Julian line, by bestowing it upon his mother Antonia, who neither by blood nor adoption was a member of that stock.' (William Sir Ramsay, *A Manual of Roman Antiquities: With Numerous Illustrations*, 1851)

'And, further, in like manner it is expedient that the case stand in regard of all things.' (Aristotle, *The Metaphysics of Aristotle. Literally Translated*, 1857)

In the light of

'The perfect frame of a man is the perfect frame of a state: and *in the light of this idea* we must read, Plato's *Republic*.' (Samuel Taylor Coleridge, *The statesman's manual*, 1816)

'In the light of this idea he will at once see the meaning of the four larger spaces into which the Table is divided, and which are separated from each other by broad circular lines.' (Thomas Worsley, *The province of the Intellect in Religion*, 1846)

'In the light of this idea, presented to man's rational consciousness, lies the whole revolutionizing power.' (*Centenary of the New Jerusalem: Twelve Addresses*, 1859)

In the same fashion

'Thus, on the Place des Gens d'Artnes, stand the opera-house, the theatre, and two gorgeous churches, all in the same fashion; the university, too, is nearly the same thing.' (*Constable's miscellany of original and selected publications*, 1828)

'With me, who, for the last two years, had seldom passed many nights together in the same room, or in the same fashion, the sharper points of my sensitiveness had become blunted by hard fare; and, provided I was not annoyed by the insect tribe, or confined by air, I slept quite as well dressed or undressed, on the ground or on a feather bed.' (George Robinson, *Three years in the East: being the substance of a journal* ...1837)

In the same way

'In the same way Amadis was the polestar, day-star, sun of valiant and devoted knights, whom all we who fight under the banner of love and chivalry are bound to imitate.' (Cervantes, *Don Quixote*, 1605)

Like

'It is a composition of a squirrel, a hare, a rat, and a monkey, which altogether looks very like a bird.' (Horace Walpole, *Letters*, 1752)

'A husband is a mere bugbear, a snap-dragon, a monster; that is to say, if one make him so, then he is a monster indeed ; and if one do not make him so, then he behaves like a monster ; and of the two evils, by my troth [...]' (Arthur Murphy, *The Way to keep Him*, 1826)

'Who can read fairy tales like a child? Who can believe the tales of the Arabian Nights like a child? Who can fear haunted places like a child? Who can tremble at a ghost story like a child? Who can conjure up spirits in the dark like a child?' (Henry Ware, *A Discourse Preached at the Ordination of Mr. Robert C. Waterston*, 1840)

Like all

'Like all that I have written for many years, it belongs as much to her as to me [...]' (J. S. Mill, *On Liberty*, 1859)

'Like all men of genius, he delighted to take refuge in poetry from the vulgarity and irritation of business. His own verses were easy and pleasant, and might have claimed no low place among those, which the French call *vers de society*.' (Robert Huish, *Memoirs of George the Fourth*, 1830)

'Theologians, like all men who devote themselves to one special pursuit, not only lose sight of every thing else, but end by even forgetting the true end of their own reflections and researches.' (*The Monthly Chronicle*, Volume 4, 1839)

Likewise

'Sancho likewise held his peace and ate acorns, and paid repeated visits to the second wine-skin, which they had hung up on a cork tree to keep the wine cool.' (Cervantes, *Don Quixote*, 1605)

Moreover

'Moreover, it is easily conceived that individuals, who are anxious for their eternal beatitude, and listen to so many different explanations, torment their brains in order to find truth.' (Charles Taylor, The Literary Panorama and National Register, 1817)

'Moreover, we are impervious to fear.' (Virginia Woolf, 'Henry James's Ghost Stories' 1921)

'Moreover, in a hundred years, I thought, reaching my own doorstep, women will have ceased to be the protected sex. Logically they will take part in all the activities and exertions that were once denied them.' (Virginia Woolf, *A Room of One's Own*, 1929)

'Moreover, it is stated that an anatomical lecturer, at Pisa, in the year 1597, happening to hold a lighted candle near a subject he was dissecting, on a sudden set fire to the vapours that came out of the stomach he had just opened.' (Reuben Percy, _Thomas Byerley, and John Timbs, *The Mirror of Literature, Amusement, and Instruction*, 1832)

Not only ... but also

' "Not only did he not pay me," replied the lad, "but as soon as your worship had passed out of the wood and we were alone, he tied me up again to the same oak and gave me a fresh flogging, that left me like a flayed Saint Bartholomew..." ' (Cervantes, *Don Quixote*, 1605)

'The idea of an Infinite Love must be added and made supreme, in order to give us a Being who is not only above all, but also through all and in all. This is the Christian Monotheism. Mohammed teaches not only the unity but also the spirituality of God, but his idea of the divine Unity is of a numeric Unity, nor a moral unity [...] (*The Atlantic*, Volume 24, 1869)

Not to mention

'Not to mention the baffled hopes of boarding-school girls of becoming authoresses, and revelling in all the luxuries of woes and loves of their own invention; not to mention the mortal sickness of Minerva at her especial press; not to mention the fastidiousness with which publishers now eye the budding flowers of young genius, nor the clipping of every Icarus's wing, without allowing the chance of a flight; not to mention the millions of sheets, which he has caused a wet blanket to be thrown over --- ' (*Atheneum, Or, Spirit of the English Magazines*, Volume 8, 1820)

'Not to mention the Duke of Wellington, who enjoys more from the public purse of England than the annual cost of the American president and all his ministers and ambassadors and their secretaries and clerks, [...]' (William Cobbett, *Cobbett's Manchester Lectures*, 1832)

'For not to mention the inveterate prejudices arising from immemorial opinions and practices, as well as from mistaken interest, which the first preachers of Christianity had to encounter, not to mention the universal contempt and detestation wherein the nation to which they belonged was holden, both by the Greeks and the Romans, not to mention the apparent ridicule and absurdity there was in exhibiting to the world as a saviour and mediator with God, a Jew [...]' (George Campbell, *Lectures on Ecclesiastical History*, 1807)

Of course

'Besides, Russia is, more than ever, the preponderating power of the North. Of course it is, that Prussia still leans upon France, is more than ever afraid to provoke her displeasure, and, perhaps, more than ever really interested in her alliance, [...]' (Fisher Ames, *Works of Fisher Ames*, 1809)

'At first, we viewed it as a misdirected but harmless effort to eradicate a principle of action, which is interwoven with the very texture of the human mind, and which, of course, it is impossible to destroy.' (*The North American Review*, 1836)

'Still there remains another grievance which is not so elementary nor so easily laid to rest; and that is, of course, the plot.' (Virginia Woolf, 'Congreve's Comedies', 1937)

'If the perspiration be clammy, of course it is a morbid secretion.' (John Elliotson, *The Principles and Practice of Medicine*, 1839)

' "She will be as well in a day or two," said Mr. Woodcourt, looking at her with an observant smile, "as she ever will be. In other words, quite well of course. Have you heard of her good fortune?" ' (Charles Dickens, *Bleak House*, 1852)

Similarly

'Similarly, the first Vatican Council decreed:' (Carl Skrade, *God and the Grotesque*, 1974, p. 41)

'Similarly, the first object which strikes one in contemplating a man is his person, the cast of his countenance, the make and proportion of his limbs, the form of his body.' Edward Meyrick Goulburn, *Sermons preached on different occasions*, 1866)

'And, similarly, the first endowments by which learning was encouraged (and academical antiquaries inform us that they are fragments of larger donations), were bestowed on the corporation, or assigned [...]' (James E. Thorold Rogers, *Education In Oxford: Its method, Its aids, and its rewards*, 1861)

So also

'For they that are discontented under Monarchy, call it Tyranny; and they that are displeased with Aristocracy, called it Oligarchy: so also, they which find themselves grieved under a Democracy, call it Anarchy, which signifies want of government. (Thomas Hobbes, *Leviathan*, 1651)

Together with

'Unfortunately, however, together with this spirit of lawful independence, of rational liberty, — together with this just, noble, and generous democracy, there has ever been another accompanying it, and forming with it the most lively contrast.' (Jaime Luciano Balmes, *European Civilisation: Protestantism and Catholicity compared*, 1855)

'Together with this aggregation of minerals in the upper ore shoot of the Western Utah mine there was apparently a considerable amount of copper in the form of copper arsenates.' (*U.S. Geological Survey*, 1935)

'Together with this advantage in large-scale production methods are the attendant reduction in the number of laborers used and hence the decreased risks in furnishing credit advances to tenants.' (United States Bureau of Labor Statistics, *Handbook of Labor Statistics*, Volumes 1-2, 1942)

To say nothing of

'To say nothing of the King's sister the Duchess of Orleans being poisoned, nor what was the occasion of it: to say nothing of the Queen Mother and Prince Rupert's leaving the Court in discontent: to say nothing of the thousands that died of the plague: to say nothing of the conflagration of London [...]' (William Hylton Dyer Longstaffe, *Memoirs of the life of Mr. Ambrose Barnes, late merchant ...*, 1867)

'Though the evil of slavery to the master be less terrible, it is not less real. And here again, to say nothing of the dread of plots and insurrections that must occasionally cross the mind; to say nothing of the habitual absence of that joyous feeling of security, that springs from a conscious interchange of benefits among the different classes of a free community; to say nothing of the chilling thought that we derive our food and raiment from the reluctant toil of fellow creatures who surround us in the capacity of slaves, by whom our persons are abhorred, and whose fears are the only tenure by which even life is held; to say nothing of these things, it is as little conducive to virtue as to happiness, to be placed in circumstances where power, may be abused with impunity, and injury inflicted without resistance.' (*African Colonization. Proceedings, on the Formation of the New-York State Colonization Society*, 1829)

Too

' – could those terms he heard by the Roman slave in the primitive church, and not make his bosom swell and glow with the idea that he too was a man, that he too was free, that he too was comprehended in "the redemption which was in Christ Jesus?" ' (John Relly Beard, *The Life of Toussaint L'Ouverture: The Negro*

Patriot of Hayti, 1853)

'There was one, however, who went home sad at heart that day, and could not lightly regard the warning. He too was a man of business, and it was the greatest possible favour to get him home early, or induce him to relax even once a year.' (*The Tract Magazine; or, Christian miscellany*, 1862)

5. THE ART OF CONTRAST AND DIFFERENCE

Many words and phrases are deployed by writers to indicate a *contrast* between people, things or ideas. The English language provides many examples to signal the notion of *difference*.

The most common examples are: above all, after all, albeit, and still, and yet, although, although this may be true, at the same time, be that as it may, besides, but, conversely, despite, different from, even so, even though, however, in contrast, in reality, in spite of, instead, nevertheless, nonetheless, notwithstanding, on the contrary, on the other hand, or, otherwise, rather, regardless of, still, then again, unlike, whereas, while, yet.

As we have been noting throughout this book, it is worth recalling that the words listed are sometimes employed at the beginning, and sometimes within a sentence. But the rules are not absolutely fixed which means that writers must use their ears when composing paragraphs. Although we are often told not to begin a sentence with the word however, this will be found not to the rule observed by many respected writers. That said, transition words and phrases are often less intrusive when they are placed inside the sentence.

Examples of the Art of Contrast and Difference

Above all

'Above all, the fine suffusion through the whole, with the characteristic manners and feelings, of a highly bred gentleman gives life to the drama.' (Coleridge, *Biographia Literaria*, 1817)

'The air faint with the perfume of orange- flower and violet, jessamine and myrtle; but, above all, the scent of the violet prevails. All is so still that even the feathery olive-leaf scarcely seems to stir.' (Charles Dickens, *All the Year Round: A Weekly Journal*, Volume 17, 1867)

'Above all, the whiskers should never be curled, nor pulled out to an absurd length. Still worse is it to cut them close with the scissors. The moustache should be neat and not too large, and such fopperies as cutting the points thereof, or twisting them up to the fineness of needles—though patronized by the Emperor of the French—are decidedly a proof of vanity.' (Cecil B. Hartley, *The Gentlemen's Book of Etiquette and Manual of Politeness*, 1860)

After all

'After all, concentration is the price the modern student pays for success.' (William Osler, *The Student Life*, 1931)

'And, after all, it mattered very little to herself.' (Charles Dickens, *All the Year Round*, Volume 3, 1870)

'After all it was only the old story over again. Many have done the like before, many will do it yet.' (*All for the best, a Story of quiet Life*, 1861)

Albeit

'He had a great affection for the wharf where he had encountered Florence, and for the streets (albeit not enchanting in themselves) by which they had come home.' (Charles Dickens, *Dombey and Son*, 1848)

'But Mr. Edger has not done all this with impunity. His sarcasms, and almost sneers, at churches and sects, albeit not without some justification, show that he has not quite attained to the calm elevated spirit of charity against which sects sin.' (Robert Vaughan, Henry Allon, *The British Quarterly Review*, 1870)

Although

'Although Crabbe's life, save for one dramatic revolution, was one of the least eventful in our literary history, it is by no means one of the least interesting.' (George Saintsbury, *Essays in English Literature 1780-1860*)

'Although she was lively and animated, her feelings were strong and deep, and her disposition uncommonly affectionate.' (Mary Shelley, *Frankenstein: or, The modern Prometheus*, 1818)

Although this may be true

'But although this may be true, we are disposed to believe, that the principle is applicable, to a proportionate extent, to many of the fevers of this country, which, under the supposition of nervous debility, have been erroneously treated upon the tonic and stimulant plan.' (*Edinburgh Medical and Surgical Journal*, Volume 7, 1811)

'But, although this may be true of some particular products, it may not be so of abundance of others, for some of which the demand has not advanced at all since 1500, while the supply of others has kept pace with the progressive demand [...]' (Jean Baptiste Say, *A Treatise on Political Economy*, 1821)

'Although this may be true, it is almost beyond credibility, and at any rate is a most dangerous experiment.' (*The Foreign Review*, Volume 1, 1828)

And still

'Then I would feel myself shrinking back to my straw, and still it would pursue me, and still it would seem to rustle through my cloak, and peep at me in every fold; for still it seemed to me, though my eyes were closed, and though I was in utter darkness.' (*The Romancist, and Novelist's Library*. Edited by William Hazlitt, 1840)

'Error may sometimes mingle, and be received with truth; but still it is error; and still it is pernicious.' (John Matthews, *The Divine Purpose: Displayed in the Works of Providence*, 1843)

'We all partake of it, and still it is not diminished; we all eat of it, and still it remains whole and entire.' (William Gahan, *Sermons and Moral Discourses*, 1825)

'Other peasants came and cut it down, and still it grew. The lightning struck the tree; it sent out fresh branches from the sides, and still it grew and bloomed.' (Leo Tolstoy, *The Long Exile: And*

Other Stories, 1899)

And yet

'And yet this is what he does when, in addition to determining the extent and character of disability, he gives necessary medical care. The moment he does this he becomes partial.' (*Bulletin of the United States Bureau of Labor Statistics*, 1916)

'And yet this very voice, also, while it goes through the obstructed passages, is dulled, and we seem to hear a sound rather than distinct words.' (Titus Lucretius Carus, *Lucretius On the Nature of Things*, 1898)

'And yet this single platoon captured the objective.' (Charles Trueman Lanham, *Infantry in Battle*, 1934)

'Such is the power of health, that without its cooperation every other comfort is torpid and lifeless, as the powers of vegetation without the sun. And yet this bliss is commonly thrown away in thoughtless negligence, or in foolish experiments on our own strength [...]' (Samuel Johnson, *The Rambler* 48, 1750)

At the same time

'Care has been taken in drawing up the petition to avoid those points which might give offence; but at the same time it is couched in terms strong and manly.' (*Report of the speeches delivered at the Lincoln county*, 1816)

'The resistance, where there is occasion for it, should be mild, courteous and dignified; at the same time, it should be frank and determined.' (*Sermons Preached at the Annual Election*, 1820)

Besides

'Besides, nothing can be so prejudicial to the morals of the inhabitants of country towns, as the occasional residence of a set of idle superficial young men, whose only occupation is gallantry, and whose polished manners render vice more dangerous, by concealing its deformity under gay ornamental drapery.' (Mary Wollstonecraft, *A Vindication of the Rights of Woman*, 1792)

'Besides, I had a contempt for the uses of modern natural philosophy.' (Mary Shelley, *Frankenstein: or, The modern Prometheus*, 1818)

'Besides, we must consider now, what can be so as from the beginning, not only what should be so. (John Milton, *Tetrachordon*, 1645)

Be that as it may

'Be that as it may, there is mischief in, every thing, which has a tendency to the relaxation of genuine religious principle; in every thing, which would oblige you to give up, or even to be remiss in habits, inculcated and prescribed by religion;' (*The Christian Remembrancer*, Volume 4, 1822)

Be this as it may

'Be this as it may, I take pleasure in acknowledging alike the excellence of the treatise he has written, its strictly philosophical spirit, the practical influence it must have upon the community, and, above all, the truly scientific manner...' (Albert Day, *Methomania: A treatise on Alcoholic Poisoning*, 1867)

But

'But to recommend thrift to the poor is both grotesque and insulting.' (Wilde, *The Soul of Man*)

'But O How fall'n!' (John Milton, *Paradise Lost*, 1667)

But, after all,

'But, after all, what is this metaphor called a crown, or rather what is monarchy? Is it a thing, or is it a name, or is it a fraud.' (Thomas Paine, *The Rights of Man*, 1791)

But apart from

'But apart from, and far beyond these, are the great principles of self-government, self-control, moral, social, and mental culture and elevation, and the aspirations of a wholesome, healthy ambition, all of which co-operation induces and inculcates.' (*The British Controversialist, and Literary Magazine*, 1867)

Conversely

'And conversely, the quantity of heat requisite to raise the temperature of equal masses of different bodies an equal number of thermometric degrees, is different, but specific for each body.' (Andrew Ure, *A Dictionary of Chemistry*, 1828)

'Conversely, the extension of track into thinly populated districts operates to reduce the average number of passengers carried per car mile.' (*Street and electric railways*, 1907)

Despite

'Rigmarole, however, can be a very agreeable thing in its way, and De Quincey has carried it to a point of perfection never reached by any other rigmaroler. Despite his undoubted possession of a kind of humour, it is a very remarkable thing that he rigmaroles, so far as can be made out by the application of the most sensitive tests, quite seriously, and almost, if not quite, unconsciously.' (George Saintsbury, *Essays in English Literature 1780-1860*)

'An eruption resulted, which she was advised to wash with sea water ; but despite this it passed into an ulcer as large as a fourpence, and I was sent for.' (American Journal of Dental Science, Volume 9, 1849)

Different from

'Widely different from this is the Christian's hope.' (Charles Simeon, *Helps to Composition, Or, Five Hundred Skeletons of Sermons*, 1802)

'Far different from this is the Gospel of Christ,' (*The Christian Remembrancer*, Volume 3, 1821)

'How different from this renown is that derived from arms alone!' (François-Réné Chateaubriand, *Travels in Greece, Palestine, Egypt, and Barbary*, 1812)

Even so

The gods were stronger, but not much; they had the unfair advantage of standing over the heads of men, and of wings for flight or for manoeuvring. Yet *even so, it was* clearly the opinion of Homers age, that, in a fair fight, the gods might have been liable to defeat.' (*Tait's Edinburgh Magazine*, Volume 13, 1846)

'If it has been correctly drawn, however, it appears to be slightly different from the normal forms, but even so it is hardly entitled to separate recognition.' (David White, *Shorter Contributions to General Geology*, 1917)

'Even so, it was not the business of literature to communicate such beliefs directly – to argue openly, for example, that private property is the bulwark of liberty.' (Terry Eagleton, *Literary Theory*, 1983: 26)

Even though

'Even though Mary Wollstonecraft had little or no presence in history or literature curricula as recently as a generation ago, she has never exactly been a minor figure. Some, certainly, have wished her so.' (Claudia L. Johnson, Introduction, *The Cambridge Companion to Mary Wollstonecraft*, 2002)

However

'However, as she at once proceeded with her dictation, and as I interrupted nothing by doing it, I ventured quietly to stop poor Peepy as he was going out and to take him up to nurse.' (Charles Dickens, *Bleak House*, 1852 'However, in his grotesque use of language, it is not Ionesco's sole purpose simply to have us experience the inadequacy of the rationalist approach.' (Carl Skrade, *God and the Grotesque*, 1974, p. 139)

'However, the majority of women are neither harlots nor courtesans; nor do they sit clasping pug dogs to dusty velvet all through the summer afternoon.' (Virginia Woolf, *A Room of One's Own*, 1929)

In contrast

'In contrast with his obedience, I learned my own disobedience; in contrast with his humility, I learned my own pride; in contrast with his compassion and the swelling of his heart with tenderness, I learned how cold and unfeeling was my own spirit.' (*The American Biblical Repository*, 1839)

In reality

'Hand dressing is not recommended for common scab; in fact, it must be looked upon as directly responsible for a considerable amount of the disease, since it is too often relied upon to cure the disease, while in reality it is only a palliative.' (*Scab in Sheep*, 1903)

'A structure in the limestone which is best exemplified here simulates an anticline or arch. In reality it is neither. It has been formed by the relative elevation of a part of the limestone above its normal position down the dip, on a plane which cuts it roughly parallel to the strike and dips southwestward.' (*United States Geological Survey*, 1905)

'The Latin, which succeeded the French for the entry and enrolment of pleas, and which continued in use for four centuries, answers so nearly to the English (oftentimes word for word) that it is not at all surprising it should generally be imagined to he totally fabricated at home, with little more art or trouble, than by adding Roman terminations to English words. Whereas in reality it is a very universal dialect, spread throughout all Europe at the irruption of the northern nations, and particularly accommodated and moulded to answer all the purposes of the lawyers with a peculiar exactness and precision. This is principally owing to the simplicity, or (if the reader pleases) the poverty and baldness of its texture, calculated to express the ideas of mankind just as they arise in the human mind, without any rhetorical flourishes, or perplexed ornaments of style [...]' (William Blackstone, *Commentaries on the Laws of England*, Volume 2, 1827)

In spite of

'The revolution of 1830 did not stop where the Duke of Wellington hoped it would have done. It has gone on much farther than he anticipated when he resolved on recognising it; and though it would have gone on more rapidly, I admit, if that recognition had not taken place, still it is going on in spite of the opposition of the Court —in spite of the efforts of the new dynasty to prevent it—in spite of reactions and reactionary laws—in spite of the hatred felt for popular rights and popular opinions by the men who govern France—and in spite of millions of obstacles thrown in its way by the men both of the old and of the new regime.' (*Tait's Edinburgh Magazine*, Volume 1, 1834)

'In spite of the importance of the visual media and performing arts as vehicles of ideas in this period, it is clear that the printed word occupied a unique position in the transmission of ideas.' (Dorinda Outram, *The Enlightenment*, 1995: 18)

Instead

'Instead, it is seen that they are used simply to show that the affections and passions, which are the real occasions of sin, are to be suppressed and eradicated in a manner as stern, self-denying, and effective for them, as the excision or eradication of an important bodily organ would be, were that the necessary means of avoiding transgression.' (David Nevins Lord, *The characteristics and laws of figurative language*, 1854)

'Instead, literature should convey *timeless* truths, thus distracting the masses from their immediate commitments, nurturing in them a spirit of tolerance and generosity, and so ensuring the survival of private property.' (Terry Eagleton, *Literary Theory*, 1983: 26)

Nevertheless

'Nevertheless, it is scarcely probable that the primitive nucleus of Etna will ever wholly disappear.' (*Graham's American Monthly Magazine*, 1853)

'Nevertheless it is as well to fall neither into one excess nor the other.' (*The Sporting Magazine*, 1845)

'Nevertheless, the presence of the products which appear in acute peri-encephalitis ought to be allowed the same significance as that of the products observed in cases of inflammation which has persisted for months.' (The American Journal of Insanity, Volume 21, 1864)

'Nevertheless, if we are urgently pressed to give some critical account of them, we may, we may safely, perhaps, venture on laying down, not indeed how and why the characters arise, but where and in what they arise.' (Matthew Arnold, *The Study of Poetry*, 1880)

Nonetheless

'Nonetheless, it is the far-seeing group which is hopefully looking forward and planning for the time when our soldiers will come home, different men from when they left us, and it will be our job to attempt to help them fit into civilian life once again.' (*Marketing Series*, 1841)

'Nonetheless this problem remains to be settled.' (*Pamphlets on Biology*, 1816)

'So, too, society has its laws—none the less real, because less obvious, to the superficial observer; none the less fixed and constant, because they relate to restless elements, which acknowledge no control; often more intricate and obscure, yet none the less to be sought after, and when ascertained, none the less to be practically relied upon, because, in their mysterious supremacy, they still leave room for an almost endless variety of phenomena.' (*The Yale Literary Magazine*, Volumes 12-13, 1847)

Notwithstanding the

'Notwithstanding this, the town must increase, and enjoys considerable trade, as it is surrounded by a good farming country, prairie and woodland, with abundance of limestone and sandstone in its vicinity.' (Eliza R. Steele, *A Summer Journey in the West*, 1841)

'Notwithstanding the many disturbing causes which interfere with first and hasty experiments of this kind, and produce results which occasionally cross and contradict each other, still there are very striking considerations which arise in comparing the gases with each other at the same temperature.' (Faraday, *Electricity*, 1847)

On the contrary

'But if, on the contrary, it is the wish of the operator to preserve the flavour or bouquet of the wine, it is necessary that the period of fermentation should be shortened.' (John MacCulloch, *Remarks on the Art of Making Wine*, 1817)

'On the contrary, government in a well-constituted republic, requires no belief from man beyond what his reason can give.' (Thomas Paine, *The Rights of Man*, 1791)

'Clearly her mind has by no means "consumed all impediments and become incandescent." On the contrary, it is harassed and distracted with hates and grievances.' (Virginia Woolf, *A Room of One's Own*, 1929)

On the other hand

'On the other hand the act of revision, the act of seeing it again, caused whatever I looked at on any page to flower before me as into the only terms that honourably expressed it;' (Henry James, *The Golden Bowl*, 1904)

'On the other hand, we may feel sure that any variation in the least degree injurious would be rigidly destroyed.' (Darwin, *The Origin of Species*, 1859)

Or

'Hence, he can say the atonement is human, or, it is not human; it is divine, or, it is not divine.' (*Gospel Advocate and Impartial Investigator*, Volume 6, 1828)

'The blind are bold, they do not see the precipice they despise. —Or perhaps there is less unwillingness to quit a world which has so often disappointed them, or which they hare sucked to the last dregs. They leave life with less reluctance, feeling that they have exhausted all its gratifications. - Or it is a disbelief of the reality of the state on which they are about to enter.—Or it is a desire to be released from excessive pain, a desire naturally felt by those who calculate their gain, rather by what they are escaping from, than by what they are to receive.—Or it is equability of temper, or firmness of nerve, or hardness of mind.—Or it is the arrogant wish to make the last act of life confirm its preceding professions.—Or it is the vanity of perpetuating their philosophic character. —Or if some faint ray of light break in, it is the pride of not retracting the sentiments which from pride they have maintained [...]' (Hannah More, *The Works of Hannah More: With a Sketch of Her Life*, Volume 1, 1827)

Or rather

'Or rather, he might seem to be like Socrates in the allegory, alternately influenced by a good and a malevolent demon; the former marking his course with actions of splendour and dignity; while the latter, mastering human frailty by means of its prevailing foible, the love of self, debased the history of a hero, by actions and sentiments worthy only of a vulgar tyrant.' (Walter Scott, *The Life of Napoleon Buonaparte, Emperor of the French*, 1834)

Other than this

'Other than this, there could be nothing actually observed, for other than this there is nothing to observe; and the additional and nobler qualities gratuitously given must have been given in consequence of a disposition in men in a rude state to attribute every virtue to those who were powerful enough to destroy even though the power was used for working destruction in the most cruel and atrocious manner.' (*The British Cyclopaedia of the Arts, Sciences, History, Geography*, 1838)

Otherwise

'First. Is the effect produced in a way which is actually and substantially different from the old way? for otherwise it is a mere repetition, and may be a mere device to avoid the old patent. Second. If the same thing be done in a new way, is it done in a better way? because otherwise it is no improvement.' (*The new American Cyclopaedia: a Popular Dictionary...*, Volume 13, 1861)

'Ours is a free monarchy — and it is of the essence of such a government, that the king can call for the services of all his liege subjects, otherwise it is not a monarchy ; and no class of subjects can be excluded from privileges, otherwise it is not a free monarchy.' (Andrew Kippis, _William Godwin, *The New Annual Register, Or General Repository of History, ...*, 1823)

Rather

'Rather than this, may Britain be
Blotted from living memory;
Rather than this, may ruin rend
This solid globe from end to end;
Rather than this, ye rolling spheres,
For ever close our mortal years,
And loud proclaim with Him of yore,
That guilty "Time shall be no more." '

(William Stokes, *The Olive Branch...*, 1860)

Regardless of

'But here is a man defying the action of the Senate, defying the express letter of the law [...] regardless of the action of the Senate, regardless of the law regulating the tenure of civil offices, regardless of the Constitution, regardless of his oath, regardless of the rights of the American people.' (Benjamin Perley Poore, *Trial of Andrew Johnson: President of the United States*, Volume 1, 1868)

'Now, if you wish to shun their fatal error, this evil must be traced to its source, and, regardless of the fears of the timid—regardless of the suggestions of a spurious liberality—and regardless of the violence of roused error, you should seek to purify our seminaries of education from that false science which misled the youth of former ages.' (*The Orthodox Presbyterian*, Volume 4, 1832)

'What is the consequence? The states of Maine and Massachusetts, regardless of the pending negociation, regardless of the common customs of national intercourse, regardless of the authority of the general government of which they are federalists, these states have themselves taken actual possession, sovereign possession of the disputed territory.' (*The Monthly Magazine*, 1827)

Still

'Still, you may object, why do you attach so much importance to this writing of books by women when, according to you, it requires so much effort, leads perhaps to the murder of one's aunts, will make one almost certainly late for luncheon, and may bring one into very grave disputes with certain very good fellows?' (Virginia Woolf, *A Room of One's Own*, 1929)

Then again

'Then, again, it is said, that he employed the very same arguments that the lecturer himself was wont to produce and refute. What then?' (*Fraser's Magazine*, Volume 5, 1832)

'Then, again, it is desirable to have long and tortuous flues, to extricate as much heat as possible from the fuel and the products of combustion;' (Richard Dennis Hoblyn, *A Manual of the Steam Engine*, 1842)

'Then, again, it is not only hard and secret, but this returning upon a man's self, it presents to a man a spectacle that is unwelcome. If a man consider his own ways, it will present to him a terrible object.' (Richard Sibbes, *The Complete Works of Richard Sibbes*,

Volume 6, 1863)

Unlike

'And yet the man who thus swayed the minds of his fellow-citizens was the very reverse of what we commonly call a demagogue. Unlike his aristocratic rival, Cimon, he never won their favour by indiscriminate bounty. Unlike his democratic successor, Cleon, he never influenced their passions by coarse invectives. Unlike his kinsman, Alcibiades, he never sought to dazzle them by a display of his genius or his wealth.' (Dawson William Turner, Heads of an Analysis of the History of Greece: For the Use of Students, 1860)

Whereas

'Whereas, all political power is inherent in the people, and governments to be permanent and satisfactory, should emanate from the same ; and, Whereas, The inhabitants of all newly settled countries and territories, who have become acquainted with their climate, cultivated their soil [...]' (*The Latter-Day Saints' Millennial Star*, Volume 12, 1850)

'Whereas the vicar, dark and dry and small beside her husband, had yet a quickness and a range of being that made Brangwen, in his large geniality, seem dull and local.' (D. H. Lawrence, *The Rainbow*, 1915)

While

'While I cannot be regarded as a pillar, I must be regarded as a buttress of the church, because I support it from the outside.' (Lord Melbourne 1779-1848)

'While every possible care has been taken to bring the most important and permanent subjects of thoughtful polemics before the minds of our readers, those matters of popular and pressing interest which occupy the serious consideration of thinking men have not been lost sight of in our more elaborate *Debates*...' (*The British Controversialist, and Literary Magazine*, 1867)

Yet

'You may drive out nature with a pitchfork, yet she'll be constantly running back (Horace, *Ars Poetica*)

'This act was in force for the remainder of his reign; those who opposed it were to suffer death;—*yet this was called a reformation!*' (William Howitt, *A popular history of priestcraft in all ages and nations*, 1834)

'Yet he could be dictatorial.' (Jenny Uglow on Erasmus Darwin, in *The Lunar Men: the Friends who Made the Future*, 2003: 172)

'Yet alongside the hopeful fantasy of moral simplification and international unity embodied in the science fiction films lurk the deepest anxieties about contemporary existence.' (Susan Sontag, *Against Interpretation*, 1994: 220)

6. THE ART OF THE SUPPLEMENT

This is a short but significant chapter. It was not an afterthought!

If the writer wants to present additional or *supplementary* ideas the most common options used in the English language are:

additionally, admittedly, again, also, and, another reason, as well, besides, equally, equally important, furthermore, in addition, moreover, then again, too.

Chapter 9 further outlines in more depth the notion of the supplement as an *illustration* or *example*.

Examples of the Art of the Supplement

Additionally

'Additionally, it had become a resolution, when leaving Lancaster, as my absence would go near to break the hearts of my parents, never to break upon my worthy father's purse.' (John Joseph Henry, *An accurate and interesting account of the hardships and sufferings of that band of heroes who traversed the Wilderness in the Campaign Against Quebec in 1775*, 1812)

'Additionally, it may be noted down here, that tickling and itching, form two kinds of sensual feelings, strictly belonging to bodily feeling.' (Peter Kaufmann, *The Temple of Truth: Or the Science of Ever-progressive Knowledge ...*, 1858)

'Additionally it has merit in its cheapness and convenience; it is ever ready, is easily prepared, and simple in its application. Its use renders the surgeon in many instances quite independent of the commercial instrument-maker —' (*Transactions of the American Orthopaedic Association*, 1893)

Admittedly

'Admittedly, the present study does not afford a reliable basis for such measurement.'

(*Financial statistics of cities having a population of over 100,000*, Volume 2, United States Bureau of the Census)

Again

'Again, there are many substances which contain elements such as would be expected arrange themselves at the opposite poles of the pile, and therefore in that respect fitted for decomposition, which yet do not conduct.' (Michael Faraday, *Electricity*, 1833)

'Others, again there are, that through a pious education, common convictions, knowledge of the truth, and such like, are convinced that their present course of life is sinful and dangerous, but flatter themselves that all shall yet be well;' (James Meikle, *Solitude Sweetened: Or, Miscellaneous Meditations on Various Religious Subjects*, 1818)

'Again, there are hills of marble which will vie with any in the world: and I have seen millstones taken from the quarry not surpassed by the French burr for manufacturing of flour, being the same to all appearance.' (*Prospectus of the Missouri Iron*

Company, 1837)

Also

'Also it must be a malicious burning; otherwise it is only a trespass ; and therefore no negligence or mischance amounts to it.' (William Blackstone, *Commentaries on the laws of England: in four books*, 1836)

'Also, isn't technique capable of good and bad uses?' (Carl Skrade, *God and the Grotesque*, 1974: 50)

'Also it must often happen that various prolixities and redundancies occur in the course of an interchange of letters, which must hang as a dead weight on the progress of the narrative.' (Walter Scott, *Redgauntlet*, 1824)

'Also it must be admitted that with us the pirate spirit dwelt far far down into recent history.' (*Blackwood's Edinburgh Magazine*, Volume 112, 1872)

And

'And by the latter in consequence of the former?' (Coleridge, *Biographia Literaria*, 1817)

'Dying is a very dull, dreary affair. And my advice to you is to have nothing to do with it.' (W. Somerset Maugham)

'And *she* was very happy too. Her young heart's love had been pent up within her own breast for years.' (*Museum of Foreign Literature, Science and Art*, 1831)

Another reason

'Another reason why the hairy boy led on was because the wolf cubs continued to trot ahead of him and he felt that so long as they went on and exhibited no signs of fear whatever, it was safe for him to proceed with his followers.' (*Boys' Life*, May 1922)

'Yet another reason is the stimulus to technical advance that is given by shortage of labour.' (Nicholas Deakin, *Origins of the Welfare State: Britain's way to social security* [1945], Routledge 2000, p.11)

Another reason (given by some) is, that they think they are old enough to take upon themselves the responsibility of their own actions; which responsibility they fancy has hitherto rested upon the shoulders of their Godfathers and Godmothers. (Edward Meyrick Goulburn, *A manual of Confirmation*, 1869)

'Still another reason, and probably the most effective one, was the fear of reprisals by France.' (Ralph Simpson Kuykendall, The Hawaiian Kingdom, 1938)

'Another reason is found in the manner of shipping men. — They are shipped like bales of cotton or barrels of beef, at one dollar per head.' (*The Sailor's Magazine*, 1854)

As well as this

'But at this I can offer no judgment without knowing the matter from that side as well as this, which I should be very glad to do, that I might, if there be occasion, be better able to argue it with them here.' (William Temple, *Works*, 1770)

'And I wonder why, with your eagle's eyes, you did not espy another foul contradiction in his words as well as this, and say, that he supposes a man may walk according to the rule of holy obedience, and yet vitiate his holy faith with a lewd and wicked conversation.' (William Chillingworth, Edward Knott, *The religion of Protestants: a safe way to Salvation*, Volume 2, 1799)

'The prince's manifesto is now sold publickly, and in all languages, as well as this inclosed fine picture ; which infamous liberty they may as well take, as the prince of Orange to speak, in his manifesto, so basely and falsely, of the great belly of the Queen, and of the supposed Prince of Wales.' (James Macpherson, *Original Papers; Containing The Secret History of Great Britain*, Volume 1, 1775)

'Had all the other arts, as well as this, been less the fruits of education and study, than the happy gifts of nature, there is no doubt but there would have existed a perfect equality between men and women.' (Stéphanie Félicité Comtesse de Genlis, *Tales of the Castle: Or, Stories of Instruction and Delight*, 1785)

Besides

'Besides, we must consider now, what can be so as from the beginning, not only what should be so. (John Milton, *Tetrachordon*, 1645)

'Besides, nothing can be so prejudicial to the morals of the inhabitants of country towns, as the occasional residence of a set of idle superficial young men, whose only occupation is gallantry, and whose polished manners render vice more dangerous, by concealing its deformity under gay ornamental drapery.' (Mary Wollstonecraft, *A Vindication of the Rights of Woman*, 1792)

'Besides, I had a contempt for the uses of modern natural philosophy.' (Mary Shelley, *Frankenstein: or, The modern Prometheus*, 1818)

Equally

'Equally unsuccessful were the trials made by Ehrenberg with the indigo and gumlac of commerce, which are always contaminated with a certain quantity of white lead, a substance highly deleterious to all animals; but, at length, by employing an indigo which was quite pure, he succeeded perfectly.' (Francis Henry Egerton Bridgewater, *The Bridgewater Treatises on the Power, Wisdom and Goodness of God as manifested in the Creation*, 1836)

Equally important

'Equally important is the provision made by most good colleges today for a faculty advisor or a faculty committee to counsel foreign students -- ' (*The Rotarian*, 1942)

'Equally important is it, that their parents should enlist the consciences of their children, to secure a ready and cheerful obedience.' (*The Religious Monitor*, 1839)

'Equally important is it (and perhaps in some respects even more so) to determine the absence of pregnancy in cases where it has been supposed to exist.' (Edward Rigby, *A System of Midwifery*, 1841)

Furthermore

'Furthermore the question arises, When will the Constitution of Ninety-three, of 1793, come into action? Considerate heads surmise, in all privacy, that the Constitution of Ninety-three will never come into action.' (Thomas Carlyle, *The French Revolution: A History*, 1838)

'... and furthermore, the people do not approbate the course of said party in the affair ; and furthermore, the people of this county desire to live in peace and amity; and furthermore, the parties who acted in this affair have left us immediately, ...' (*Annual Report of the Commissioner of Indian Affairs*, 1860)

'Furthermore, the manure might be, and often is, taken from the heap where diseased plants have been thrown to compost, or it may be from animals that have fed on diseased cabbage.' (*Farmers' Bulletin*, 1869)

'Furthermore, the fine line drawn in literary studies between those works worthy of scholarly attention and inclusion in the canon and those assigned to the category of popular literature if often contingent upon the author's sex and choice of genre.' (Resa L. Dudovitz, *The Myth of Superwoman Women's Bestsellers in France and the United State*, 1990: 20)

In addition

'but the poor man is exposed to great hazard; and, in addition, it is to be feared, the conversation which goes on is seldom likely to improve his mind, or increase his loyal obedience to established authority;' (*Monthly Magazine and British Register*, 1819)

'In addition to the facts stated in the return, it was proved to the said Court, that the petitioners are citizens of the United States.' (*Decisions of the General Court of Virginia*, 1826)

'The conditions required to produce germination are, exposure to moisture, and a certain quantity of heat; in addition, it is necessary that a communication with the atmosphere should be provided, if germination is to be maintained in a healthy state.' (John Lindley, *The Theory and Practice of Horticulture*, 1855)

'In addition, it is found that the prostate, or any one of its lobes, may become enlarged; and it has become the universal belief, since the days of Sir E. Home, that stricture in the deeper portions of the canal depends upon this cause, or upon abscess in the neighborhood.' (William Acton, *Practical Treatise on Diseases of the Urinary and Generative Organs in both Sexes*, 1858)

Moreover

'Moreover, it is easily conceived that individuals, who are anxious for their eternal beatitude, and listen to so many different explanations, torment their brains in order to find truth.' (Charles Taylor, The Literary Panorama and National Register, 1817)

'Moreover, we are impervious to fear.' (Virginia Woolf, 'Henry James's Ghost Stories' 1921)

'Moreover, in a hundred years, I thought, reaching my own doorstep, women will have ceased to be the protected sex. Logically they will take part in all the activities and exertions that were once denied them.' (Virginia Woolf, *A Room of One's Own*, 1929)

'Moreover, it is stated that an anatomical lecturer, at Pisa, in the year 1597, happening to hold a lighted candle near a subject he was dissecting, on a sudden set fire to the vapours that came out of the stomach he had just opened.' (Reuben Percy, _Thomas

Byerley, and John Timbs, *The Mirror of Literature, Amusement, and Instruction*, 1832)

Then

'Quickly she started up, leaped right upwards many times; then ran to and fro with an hundred odd gesticulations. She beat herself on the head, tore her hair, and attempted to run into the fire.' (John Wesley, *The Works of the Rev. John Wesley*, 1829)

Then again

'Then, again, it is said, that he employed the very same arguments that the lecturer himself was wont to produce and refute. What then?' (*Fraser's Magazine*, Volume 5, 1832)

'Then, again, it is desirable to have long and tortuous flues, to extricate as much heat as possible from the fuel and the products of combustion;' (Richard Dennis Hoblyn, *A Manual of the Steam Engine*, 1842)

'Then, again, it is not only hard and secret, but this returning upon a man's self, it presents to a man a spectacle that is unwelcome. If a man consider his own ways, it will present to him a terrible object.' (Richard Sibbes, *The Complete Works of Richard Sibbes*, Volume 6, 1863)

Too

' – could those terms he heard by the Roman slave in the primitive church, and not make his bosom swell and glow with the idea that he too was a man, that he too was free, that he too was comprehended in "the redemption which was in Christ Jesus?"' (John Relly Beard, *The Life of Toussaint L'Ouverture: The Negro Patriot of Hayti*, 1853)

'There was one, however, who went home sad at heart that day, and could not lightly regard the warning. He too was a man of business, and it was the greatest possible favour to get him home early, or induce him to relax even once a year.' (*The Tract Magazine; or, Christian miscellany*, 1862)

7. THE ART OF DISPUTATION

In the process of disputation, *argument*, or debate a writer sometimes indicates that a point has been agreed or already taken into account.

In order to suggest that a point has been *conceded* the following words and phrases may be used: agreed, certainly, granted, obviously, of course, to be sure.

Other words or phrases may be selected in order to signal *emphasis*. Examples are: above all, chiefly, chief attribute, clearly, for the most part, more particularly, most curious, most significantly, generally, the general truth, to be more precise.

Examples of the *sequence* of ideas are illustrated in Chapter 8.

By using words associated with the language of debate the writer provides a sense of critical discussion and evaluation. It is also worth recalling the deployment of the abstract words that can be preceded with the words *this*:

account, advice, answer, argument, area, assertion, assumption, claim, comment, concept, conclusion, confusion, contradiction, criticism, critique, decrease, description, deterioration, difficulty, discussion, distinction, drawback, effect, emphasis, error, estimate, example, explanation, failing, finding, hypothesis, idea, improvement, increase, interpretation, narrative, notion, observation, paradigm, proof, proposal, reading, reference, report, setback, situation, strategy, suggestion, tactic, theory, variation, view, warning, weakness.

Examples of the Art of Disputation

Above all

'Above all, the fine suffusion through the whole, with the characteristic manners and feelings, of a highly bred gentleman gives life to the drama.' (Coleridge, *Biographia Literaria*, 1817)

'Above all, the whiskers should never be curled, nor pulled out to an absurd length. Still worse is it to cut them close with the scissors. The moustache should be neat and not too large, and such fopperies as cutting the points thereof, or twisting them up to the fineness of needles—though patronized by the Emperor of the French—are decidedly a proof of vanity.' (Cecil B. Hartley, *The Gentlemen's Book of Etiquette and Manual of Politeness*, 1860)

Agreed

'That such a defect may sometimes occur, as a chest too narrow for lungs of an uncommon extension, that constitute naturally what are called *thick-winded horses*, our author does not deny: in which cases, it is agreed, there is no hope of a cure, nor scarcely of any alleviation, But he will by no means admit the above deformity to be a case of common occurrence, far less that it is the universal or even the most ordinary cause.' (*Encyclopaedia Britannica*, Volume 7, 1810)

'Agreed; there is no moon, and but few stars; in ten minutes it will be dark as pitch.' (*Hogg's Instructor*, 1851)

Certainly

' "Certainly the best works, and of greatest merit for the public, have proceeded from the unmarried or childless men." I say the same of women.' (Lord Bacon quoted in Mary Wollstonecraft, *A Vindication of the Rights of Woman*, 1792)

'Cruikshank is certainly the most original artist of the day, at least in point of inventive faculty.' (*The Metropolitan*, 1831)

'Bossuet, certainly the most powerful of the French ecclesiastical declaimers, and Fleury, as certainly the most candid, exact, and intelligent of the French ecclesiastical historians, attack him without mercy, and charge his memory with all the excesses of religious lust of power.' (*The Foreign Monthly Review and Continental Literary Journal*, 1839)

'Certainly, as I strolled round the court, the foundation of gold and silver seemed deep enough; the pavement laid solidly over the wild grasses.' (Virginia Woolf, *A Room of One's Own*, 1929)

Chiefly

'The readers should be carried forward, not merely or chiefly by the mechanical impulse of curiosity, or by a restless desire to arrive at the final solution; but by the pleasurable activity of mind excited by the attractions of the journey itself.' (Coleridge, *Biographia Literaria*, 1817)

Chief attribute

'Its chief attribute is clearness; it has not marks to express confused notions.' (Fourier on Mathematics, in *Theory of Heat*)

Clearly

'Clearly her mind has by no means "consumed all impediments and become incandescent." On the contrary, it is harassed and distracted with hates and grievances.' (Virginia Woolf, *A Room of One's Own*)

For the most part

'And all this is, for the most part, that subtle kind of localism of which it is much easier to show the existence than to ascertain the cause.' (*The Ecclesiologist*, 1850)

'For the most part, the roads in the island are steps cut or laid in the solid rock; and our alert, sure-footed little animals, climbed them with the agility of mountain goats.' (*Southern Literary Messenger*, 1840)

General truth

'The general truth of the principle, long ago insisted on by Humboldt, that man admires and often tries to exaggerate whatever characters nature may have given him, is shown in many ways.' (Charles Darwin, *The Descent of Man*)

Generally speaking

'Generally speaking, up until about twenty years ago, historians of this period usually thought of *the* Enlightenment, as a relatively unitary phenomenon in the history of ideas…' (Dorinda Outram, *The Enlightenment*, 1995: 3)

Granted

'This being granted, it is a question of considerable importance what copy, or copies shall be used, in order to form this projected edition.' (J. B. B. Clarke, *An Account of the Infancy, Religious and Literary Life of Adam Clarke*, 1833)

'At present, let it be granted that this Society has printed or reprinted the Bible in fifty-four languages, let it be granted also that these Editions have been printed by the sole exertions of this society, let it be granted that none of them would have been printed, if this Society had not existed, let it be granted, even, that these fifty-four editions are in languages in which the Scriptures had never appeared before, and lastly, let it be granted [...]' (*The Pamphleteer*, Volume 1, 1813)

More exactly

'More exactly, what does it mean to speak of theology rooted in anthropology.' (Carl Skrade, *God and the Grotesque*, 1974, p. 14)

More particularly

'You see by the confidence I repose in you, that I have not; more particularly, on this very important occasion, in which your assistance may crown the work: for, if she waver, a little innocent contrivance will be necessary.' (Samuel Richardson, *Clarissa Harlowe*, 1748)

Most curious

'The most curious problem of all, is this truth of absurdity to itself.' (William Hazlitt, *Lectures on English Comic Writers* pp. 14-15)

Most Significantly

'Most significantly, though Mr. Lonsdale does not comment upon it, is the vivid similarity between Johnson's psychological attitude and that of Burney in his old age.' (*The Burke Newsletter*, Volumes 7-8, 1769)

'Most significantly then is my late publication entitled, "The Church in Danger from Herself."' (John Acaster, *Remedies for the Church in danger*, 1830)

'But under the sultry skies, and amidst the burning sands, of the East, it awakened exquisite emotion, and was a lively emblem of temporal and spiritual felicity. Most significantly does it depict the condition of believers.' (John Mitchell Mason, *The Writings of the Late John M. Mason, D. D.*, 1832)

Obviously

'Obviously, it is not merely the consciousness of an impression neither in theory nor in fact; equally obviously, it is the consciousness of a change, or of changes, produced in the organ of consciousness, directly or indirectly, by impressions, one or more.' (*Journal of Psychological Medicine*, Volume 4, 1851)

'Obviously it is intolerable that, at an exclusively political club, no gentleman can speak his mind freely, without taking the precaution of scanning the whole of the apartment, lest, within earshot, there may lurk some knavish underling of the other party.' (*The Living Age*, Volume 37, 1853)

'Obviously it is impossible, I thought, looking into those foaming waters, to compare them.' (Virginia Woolf, *A Room of One's Own*, 1929)

Of course

'Besides, Russia is, more than ever, the preponderating power of the North. Of course it is, that Prussia still leans upon France, is more than ever afraid to provoke her displeasure, and, perhaps, more than ever really interested in her alliance, [...]' (Fisher Ames, *Works of Fisher Ames*, 1809)

'At first, we viewed it as a misdirected but harmless effort to eradicate a principle of action, which is interwoven with the very texture of the human mind, and which, of course, it is impossible to destroy.' (*The North American Review*, 1836)

'Still there remains another grievance which is not so elementary nor so easily laid to rest; and that is, of course, the plot.' (Virginia Woolf, 'Congreve's Comedies', 1937)

'If the perspiration be clammy, of course it is a morbid secretion.' (John Elliotson, *The Principles and Pratice of Medicine*, 1839)

Particularly

'Particularly, I cannot but be pleased to observe, that although he speaks of the ladies of his family with the freedom of relationship, yet it is always of tenderness.' (Samuel Richardson, *Clarissa Harlowe*, 1748)

To be more precise

'I am glad, however, of the opportunity to be more precise on the subject, for it was in 1803, not 1804, that the parliamentary discussion occurred [..]' (*The Gentleman's Magazine*, Volumes 169-170, 1841)

'To be more precise, it is situated at the junction of the Skirden with the Ribble, three quarters of a mile south of the village of

Bolton by Bewland. It is castellated, and remarkable for its solidity even at a period when buildings were most substantial.'

(By Sir Bernard Burke, *A Visitation of the Seats and Arms of the Noblemen and Gentlemen of Great Britain,* Volume 2, 1853)

'In fact, it is an established law of steam, and of all elastic fluids generally, that the pressure which they exert is inversely as the space occupied; or, to be more precise, it is very nearly so.' (Zerah Colburn, *The Locomotive Engine: including a Description of its Structure, Rules for estimating its Capabilities ...,* 1851)

To be sure

'Well, I say nothing; but to be sure it is a pity some folks had not been better born; nay, as for that matter, I should not mind it myself; but then there is not so much money; and what of that?' (Henry Fielding, *Tom Jones,* 1749)

'To be sure it is natural for us to wish our enemies dead, that the wars may be at an end and our taxes be lowered; for it is a dreadful thing to pay as we do.' (Henry Fielding, *Tom Jones,* 1749)

'Well, to be sure, it is curious; but some such there have been, and always will be, in the gay world ; and indeed they are very amusing ; it is beyond belief how they divert one.' (Charlotte Campbell Bury, *Flirtation: a Novel,* 1827)

'To be sure, he has not a vital interest in the suit in question, her part in which was the only property my Lady brought him; and he has a shadowy impression that for his name—the name of Dedlock—to be in a cause, and not in the title of that cause, is a most ridiculous accident.' (Charles Dickens, *Bleak House,* 1852)

8. THE ART OF THE SEQUENCE

In order to provide a sense of *logical sequence* the writer uses words such as:

accordingly, as a result, because, because of, consequently, due to, even if, for fear that, for this reason, for the purpose of, forthwith, granted (that), hence, henceforth, if, in case, in order to, in that case, in the event that, in the hope that, in view of, inasmuch as, lest, on account of, on (the) condition (that), only, owing to, provided that, seeing that, since, so, so as to, so long as, so that, thereby, therefore, thereupon, thus, to the end that, under those circumstances, unless, when, whenever, while, with this in mind, with this intention.

In these examples there may be a sense of cause and effect, or the sense that one idea results from another. In some cases there is the sense of *conditionality* or a specific relation of *purpose*.

It is also worth looking back at *The Art of Timing* as that chapter also deals with the sense of sequences.

The words illustrated in this section are also close friends with the words used when creating effective discussions, arguments and evaluations. You are therefore reminded to recollect *The Art of Disputation*.

Examples of the Art of the Sequence

Accordingly

'Accordingly, it is said, that the sudden taking in of a large quantity of very cold water, has produced dropsy, probably from the cold producing a constriction of the excretories.' (William Cullen, *First Lines of the Practice of Physic*, 1816)

'Accordingly it is found, that an insulated metallic plate held in a volume of steam, is electrified positively by the condensation and conversion into water of the vapour striking upon its surface.' (James Smith, *The Panorama of Science and Art*, 1828)

'Accordingly, it is advisable, in a wise constitution of things, that the agriculturists, the labourers, and the market-people, should be kept formally distinct, as if by the institution of castes, from the military and sovereign classes, on the ground that their pursuits are degrading, and unfavourable to virtue.' (Heinrich Ritter, *The History of Ancient Philosophy*, 1839)

As a result

'As a result it does not appear that from a weights and measures standpoint the height requirement can be justified.' (Arthur Evarts Kimberly, John Frederick Gross Hicks, *A Survey of Storage Conditions in Libraries Relative to the Preservation of Records*, 1931)

'As a result 136 rats were killed during the first twenty nights, when the losses practically ceased, and the method has been continued in the store ever since with satisfactory results. Guillotine traps should be baited with small pieces of Vienna sausage (Wienerwurst) or bacon.' (David Ernest Lantz, *Methods of Destroying Rats*, 1907).

As long as

'For as long as we are the creatures of an infinite perfect Creator, it will be as much our duty as it is now to love and adore him; as long as we are reasonable creatures, it will be as much our duty as it is now to submit our will and affections to our reason; and as long as we are related to other reasonable creatures, it will be as much our duty as it is now to be kind, and just, and peaceable, in all our intercourses with them.' (John Scott, *The Works of the Learned and Reverend John Scott, D. D.*, Volume 1, 1826)

'As long as we remain in an imaginary real of being we misrecognize our identities, seeing them as fixed and rounded…'

(Terry Eagleton, *Literary Theory*, 1983: 186)

Because of this

'Because of this and because of the larger proportions of nitrogen to organic matter in the colloids, the ratios appear more certain.' (Irvin Cecil Brown and James Thorp, *Morphology and composition of some soils of the Miami family and the Miami Catena*, 1942)

'Because of this international-mindedness the Viennese during the War were themselves never stirred by the germ of hatred toward other nations.' (*The Rotarian*, 1930)

'Yet, because of this — because the telephone is so useful — the demand for service keeps growing greater.' (*The Popular Science Monthly*, 1923)

Consequently

'Consequently, each new variety or species, during the progress of its formation, will generally press hardest on its nearest kindred, and tend to exterminate them.' (Darwin, *The Origin of Species*, 1859)

Due to this

'It therefore appears to me that in every case in which scent is given off by an animal, it will in part be due to this source; and, in so far as it is due to this source, will it be of a nature corresponding to that of the scent arising from musk, or, in other words, possessing no substantiality, and so not depending upon either vapourous or molecular matters.' (*Zoologist: A Monthly Journal of Natural History*, Volume 16, 1858)

'It is due to ourselves; it is due to the President ; it is due to the country, that we should express an opinion.' (*Debates in Congress*, 1826)

'It is due to the Editors, to say that they disclaim the implied doctrine of their correspondent, in the most becoming manner.' (Parker Pillsbury, *The Church as it is: Or, The Forlorn Hope of Slavery*, 1847)

Earlier

'Earlier it could have annoyed me, but now everything was in good hands and swimming right along.' (Mark Twain, *A Connecticut Yankee in King Arthur's Court*, 1889)

'The earlier it was given in the first stage of the disease, the better. When given freely, so as to produce secretion in the liver, kidneys, and skin, a general and equable re-action soon succeeded.' (James Ewell, *The medical companion: or family physician*, 1827)

Even if

'Destructiveness always wants to be kept busy. It will keep busy, even if it is in pinching the boy next to him. Having, by some active employment, secured the attention, the teacher may call into exercise the faculty next largest to that of Destructiveness.' (John Hecker, *The Scientific Basis of Education: Demonstrated by an Analysis of the Temperaments and of the Phrenological Facts*, 1867)

For fear that

'And who was the man on this floor that was afraid to read the reasons urged by a committee which this body had selected to consider a subject, for fear that he should get information and be convinced?' (*Report of the Debates and Proceedings of the Convention for the Revision of the Constitution of New York State*, 1846)

'She must not go across the brook, for fear that she might get lost in the woods, nor go out of sight of the house in any direction.' (Jacob Abbott, *Mary Erskine: A Franconia Story*, 1850)

For this reason

'While he enjoyed liberty, the regent could not reckon his own power secure. For this reason, having by an artifice allured Maitland to Stirling, he employed Captain Crawford, one of his creatures, to accuse him of being accessory to the murder of the king; and under that pretence he was arrested and carried as a prisoner to Edinburgh.' (William Robertson, *The History of Scotland during the Reign of Queen Mary and of King James VI*, 1836)

'They aimed at bringing about a change in the religion, and a revolution in the government of the kingdom. For this reason they solicited the aid of the king of Spain, the avowed and zealous patron of popery in that age.' (William Robertson, *The History of Scotland during the Reign of Queen Mary and of King James VI*, 1836)

For the purpose of

'The breaking up of a street, whenever it takes place, whether it be for the purpose of water, gas, sewers, or whatever it may be, is always an annoyance amounting to a nuisance.' (*The Law Journal*, 1869)

Forthwith

'Forthwith he gave in charge unto his Squire,

That scarlot whore to keepen carefully;
Whiles he himselfe with greedie great desire
Into the Castle entred forcibly.' (Edmund Spenser, *The Faerie Queene*, Book 1, Canto 8: 29, 1590)

'Forthwith he made the well his objective. In that country wells were not plentiful.' (Oscar Micheaux, *The Homesteader: A Novel*, 1917)

Granted

'This being granted, it is a question of considerable importance what copy, or copies shall be used, in order to form this projected edition.' (J. B. B. Clarke, *An Account of the Infancy, Religious and Literary Life of Adam Clarke*, 1833)

'At present, let it be granted that this Society has printed or re-printed the Bible in fifty-four languages, let it be granted also that these Editions have been printed by the sole exertions of this society, let it be granted that none of them would have been printed, if this Society had not existed, let it be granted, even, that these fifty-four editions are in languages in which the Scriptures had never appeared before, and lastly, let it be granted [...]' (*The Pamphleteer*, Volume 1, 1813)

Hence

'Hence, the struggle for the production of new and modified descendents will mainly lie between larger groups which are all trying to increase in number.' (Charles Darwin, *The Origin of Species*, 1859)

'Hence, perhaps, the peculiar nature of woman in fiction; the astonishing extremes of her beauty and horror; her alternations between heavenly goodness and hellish depravity — for so a lover would see her as his love rose or sank, was prosperous or unhappy.' (Virginia Woolf, *A Room of One's Own*, 1929)

'Hence, prating peasant! fetch thy master home.' (William Shakespeare, Comedy of Errors)

'Hence! home, you idle creatures get you home! Is this a holiday?' (William Shakespeare, *Julius Caesar*)

Henceforth

'Henceforth it will therefore be restricted to an outline of events, and, in each successive presidency, attention will be principally directed to the nature and objects of the Professorships established or enlarged.' (*The North American Review*, 1841)

'Henceforth it will dedicate to its Creator all its thoughts, memories, hopes, feelings, affections. Henceforth it will seek, above all things, not for its own happiness, but for His glory.' (*The Metropolitan*, 1846)

'Henceforth it never for a moment yielded to the efforts of her physicians — physicians, who combined profound knowledge of their profession, with the liberal, warm and tender sensibilities of men.' (Thomas Peabody Grosvenor, *A Sketch of the Life, Last Sickness, and Death of Mrs. Mary Jane Grosvenor*, 1817)

If

'If people knew as much about painting as I do, they would never buy my pictures.' (Edwin Landseer 1802-1873)

'If we may be excused the antithesis, we should say that eloquence is heard, poetry is overheard.' (John Stuart Mill, *Thoughts on Poetry and Its Varieties*, 1859)

'If music be the food of love, play on,' (William Shakespeare, *Twelfth Night, or What You Will*)

'If you shall chance, Camillo, to visit Bohemia,' (William Shakespeare, *The Winter's Tale*)

If all

'If all fools wore white caps, we should look like a flock of geese.' (John Wade, *Select Proverbs*, 1824)

If the truth were known

'If the truth were known the most disagreeable people are the most amiable.' (William Hazlitt's 'On Good Nature,' 1816)

'If the truth were known, some of the ruddy-faced dairy wenches might perhaps call him a damnation rogue, as justly as their betters of the same sex might Squire Lovelace.' (Richardson, *Clarissa*)

If this be so

'If this be so, the sooner such a civilization receives notice to quit, the better.' (J. S. Mill, *On Liberty*, 1859)

In order to

'In order to make it clear how, as I believe, natural selection acts, I must beg permission to give one or two imaginary illustrations.'

(Darwin, *The Origin of Species*, 1859)

'In order to know the manner of their formation, it will be proper to divide them into separate classes, according to the different feats where they are formed, whether the lips, teeth, palate, or nose; thence denominated, labial, dental, palatine, and nasal.' (Thomas Sheridan, *A General Dictionary of the English Language*, 1780)

In the event of

'In the event of the absolute necessity of repelling hostility for self-preservation, it will certainly be more consonant to humanity, and perhaps more effectual in striking terror, that the first guns fired be only loaded with small shot.' (James Tuckey, *Narrative of an expedition to explore the river Zaire*, 1816)

In the hope that

'There can be no doubt, that the great men whose names have been mentioned, patronized the Colonization Society especially in the hope that gradually, but rapidly, it would tend to deliver the country from the incubus of slavery, in a way to which no one could have any right or reason to object.'(Nathan Lewis Rice, *Lectures on Slavery: Delivered in the North Presbyterian Church, Chicago*, 1860)

'I plunged about in several directions, but I could discover no traces of my advance; and in despair I started off, haphazard, into the leafy labyrinth, now and then stopping to shout, in the hope that my voice might reach the ears of some of my party.' (Mrs. Henry Wood, *The Argosy*, Volume 5, 1901)

In view of this

'In view of this fact and in View of all the circumstances surrounding this case, the chairman believes that in the interest of fair dealing, A should be reinstated either in his former position, or in some other of equal advantage.' (Charles Henry Winslow, _Royal Meeker, *Collective Agreements in the Men's Clothing Industry*, 1916)

'In view of this situation, the Forester, early in 1917, commissioned the writer to make an extended examination in the field and to report to him as to existing conditions of recreation, with recommendations of methods and general policies.' (United States. Forest Service, Frank Albert Waugh, *Recreation Uses on the National Forests*, 1918)

Inasmuchas

'Inasmuch as the general considerations to be brought forward have respect to those great forces of the globe, exerted by it, both as mass and through its particles, namely magnetism and gravitation, it is necessary briefly to recall certain relations and differences of the two which have been insisted upon on former occasions.' (Faraday, *Observations on the Magnetic Force*, 1853)

'Inasmuch then as the theology of Christianity did not appear to him true or of divine origin; inasmuch as this strange history of a crucified God was not credible to him, and a system which purported to rest entirely upon a foundation to him so wholly unbelievable, could not be foreseen by him to be that renovating agency which, after all abatements, it has in fact proved to be; the gentlest and most amiable of philosophers and rulers, under a solemn sense of duty, authorized the persecution of Christianity.' (J. S. Mill, *On Liberty*, 1859)

Lest

'Lest the half-lifeless charmer should catch cold in this undress, I lifted her to her bed, and sat down by her upon the side of it, endeavouring with the utmost tenderness, as well of action as expression, to dissipate her terrors.' (Samuel Richardson, *Clarissa Harlowe*, 1748)

On account of

'It was on account of this circumstance, principally, that the present narrative was prefixed to a relation of experiments in which the Specific Gravity of a Metallic substance was changed by a minute proportion of a powder [...]' (James Price, *An Account of some Experiments on Mercury, Silver and Gold*, 1782)

'On account of this condition, some difficulty is experienced in preparing the land for crops during early spring.' (*United States Soil Conservation Service: Soil Survey Reports*, 1930)

On the condition that

'Therefore, in a devise in fee-simple, on the condition that the devisee do not alien, the condition is void.' (William Roberts, *A Treatise on the Law of Wills and Codicils*, Volume 2, 1823) -

'They will say, in a moment, that the Mingo of the Chickasaws is a monarch, who, in his great condescension, has granted the humble request of the President, on the condition that the petitioner shall make a pecuniary compensation, and pay tribute, under the name of ferriage, to the Chickasaws, as often as any of the President's people pass through the territory of the king of the Chickasaws.' (Jeremiah Evarts, *Essays on the Present Crisis in the Condition of the American Indians*, 1829)

Owing to this

'Owing to this, we left Fort Washington strongly garrisoned in our rear, when we were obliged to retreat to White Plains ; and owing to this, also, Colonel Magaw, who commanded at it, was ordered to defend it to the last extremity.' (*The Writings of George Washington*, 1835)

Provided that

'Provided that we may have equal hearing, I am content to yield, though I declare, You have no power to judge us.' (John Dryden, *Amboyna*, 1673)

Seeing that

'Seeing that he performeth so much for his friends, and his enemies, yet being together, what shall he do for his friends separately! Seeing that he comforteth us so much in the day of tears, how much shall he comfort us in the day of marriage! Seeing that the prison containeth such things, what manner of things shall our country contain!' (*Writings of Edward the Sixth, William Hugh, Queen Catherine Parr, Anne Askew ...*, 1836)

'Seeing that he was desirous to make some further communication to me, I cautioned him of the possible consequences, and begged him, if he had made any communication to Dr. Forrester, or wished to make any further one to me, under the impression that he would be admitted a witness for the crown, to dismiss the expectation from his mind.' (Edmund Burke, ed., *Annual Register*, Volume 76, 1835)

Since

'Since the death of her aunt, her mind had acquired new firmness and vigour.' (Mary Shelley, *Frankenstein: or, The modern Prometheus*, 1818)

So

'So he wrote, as it were, his name.' (Henry James, *The Golden Bowl*, 1904)

'So wit is often the more forcible and pointed for being dry and serious, for it then seems as if the speaker himself had no intention in it, and we were the first to find out.' (William Hazlitt, *Lectures on English Comic Writers*, 1819)

'So, in the name of health and sanity, let us not dwell on the end of the journey.' (Virginia Woolf, 'Montaigne' in *The Common Reader*, 1925)

'This great Nation will endure as it has endured, will revive and will prosper. So, first of all, let me assert my firm belief that the only thing we have to fear is fear itself - nameless, unreasoning, unjustified terror which paralyzes needed efforts to convert retreat into advance.' (Franklin D. Roosevelt, *First Inaugural Address*, 1933)

So also

'For they that are discontented under Monarchy, call it Tyranny; and they that are displeased with Aristocracy, called it Oligarchy: so also, they which find themselves grieved under a Democracy, call it Anarchy, which signifies want of government. (Thomas Hobbes, *Leviathan*, 1651)

So as

'Work expands so as to fill the time available for its completion.' (Parkinson's Law, 1958)

So that

'The heat increasing within the marrow, his eyes fell out of his head, so that he utterly lost his sight. Being in this miserable state, he confessed himself overtaken, calling for death, and acknowledging it was the just recompense of his fury, and insolence against Christ.' (Nathaniel Wanley, *The Wonders of the Little World: Or, A General History of Man...*, Volume 1, 1806)

'But patient, firm, diligent training by-and-by subdues him, so that he becomes docile. His original frantic efforts become nimbleness and fine action. He is not changed so that he has other than a quick, sensitive disposition; but his quickness and sensitiveness are disciplined, so that he is steady and easily manageable. He is broken not in his absolute nature, but in the way in which he carries that nature, which is tantamount to the eradication of it.' (*Water-cure Journal*, Volume 48, 1869)

So then

' "So then," said Sancho, "it would be entirely of your own choice you would keep from sleeping; not in opposition to my will?" ' (Cervantes, *Don Quixote*, 1605)

' "So then, senora," said Sancho, "no other mishap has befallen you, nor was it jealousy that made you leave home, as you said at the beginning of your story?" ' (Cervantes, *Don Quixote*, 1605)

' "So then," said Sancho, munching hard all the time, "your worship does not agree with the proverb that says, 'Let Martha die, but let her die with a full belly.'" '(Cervantes, *Don Quixote*, 1605)

' "So then, senora, you are the fair Dorothea, the only daughter of the rich Clenardo?" '(Cervantes, *Don Quixote*, 1605)

Thereby

'Or whether there are among the Hong Merchants some worthless vagabonds, who have brooked to flatter, thereby leading to the Foreigners presuming to perform this act of non-conformity to old usage?' (Parliamentary Papers, House of Commons, 1832)

'By degrees they fill the cavity of the viscus, and by pressing on the orifices of the ureters prevent the descent of the urine into the bladder, thereby leading to dilatation of these ducts, and eventually to disease of the kidney.' (*The Dublin Quarterly Journal of Medical Science*, 1860)

Therefore

'Therefore it is that, throughout all the seven books of an enquiry into "Popular Errors," by a man of singular acuteness, enlightened by singular learning, no searching comment attends a single error directly injurious to the political or social happiness of mankind. Therefore it is that the enquirer himself, while professing to expose the blunders of the people, disdainfully boasts, that *for* the people, "whom books do not redress," his work is not intended. Therefore it is that, throughout all our author's gravest and loftiest idealism, there is (beyond the affectation and quaintness of the day) something of the whimsical frivolity of a man who lives alone, with no occupation so attractive as that of sporting with his own fancies, and caressing his own conceits. Therefore it is that, while Sir Thomas Browne will always command the admiration of poets, and the respect of scholars, he will find, we fear, the justice of retaliation in the indifference of the ordinary public.' (*The Edinburgh Review Or Critical Journal*, Volume 44, 1836)

'Therefore, while Mr. Tulkinghorn may not know what is passing in the Dedlock mind at present, it is very possible that he may.' (Charles Dickens, *Bleak House*, 1852)

Thereupon

'Thereupon the duke seized the opportunity of practising this mystification upon him; so much did he enjoy everything connected with Sancho and Don Quixote.' (Cervantes, *Don Quixote*, 1605)

Thus

'Thus, as I believe, natural selection will tend in the long run to reduce any part of the organisation, as soon as it becomes, through changed habits, superfluous, without by any means causing some other part to be largely developed in a corresponding degree.' (Darwin, *The Origin of Species*, 1859)

'Thus, in peace and gaiety, glided the days of my childhood.' (Mary Hays, *Memoirs of Emma Courtney*)

'Thus she gave him, standing off a little, the firmest longest deepest injunction he had ever received from her.' (Henry James, *The Golden Bowl*, 1904)

'Thus rumour thrives in the capital, and will not go down into Lincolnshire.' (Charles Dickens, *Bleak House*, 1852)

To the end that

'And, to the end that it may be the better known whether any ship or vessel be actually infested with the plague, or other infectious disease or distemper as aforesaid, or whether such ship or vessel, or the mariners or passengers coming, or the cargo imported in the fame, are liable to any orders touching quarantine;' (*The Statutes at Large from the Magna Charta ... to 1761*, 1805)

Under those circumstances

'Under those Circumstances, it is possible it might take a Quarter of an Hour? Yes; but there are Times when they would not be able to go by at all, when it is blowing hard. Would they pole under those Circumstances?' (*House of Lords: The Sessional Papers 1801-1833*)

'Q. Under those circumstances, in justice to the Board, should not your statement that the Water Board would not deal with you honest men while you were the owners of the land, be somewhat modified?' (*Documents of the City of Boston*, 1886)

Unless

'Unless, indeed, when society in general is in so backward a state that it could not or would not provide for itself any proper institutions of education, unless the government undertook the task; then, indeed, the government may, as the less of two great evils, take upon itself the business of schools and universities, as it may that of joint-stock companies, when private enterprise, in a shape fitted for undertaking great works of industry, does not exist in the country.' (J. S. Mill, *On Liberty*, 1859)

When

'When a man assumes public trust, he should consider himself as public property.' (Thomas Jefferson)

'When we survey the wretched condition of man under monarchical and hereditary systems of government, dragged from his home by one power, or driven by another, and impoverished by taxes more than by enemies, it becomes evident that those systems are bad, and that a general revolution in the principle and construction of governments is necessary.' (Thomas Paine, *The Rights of Man*, 1791)

'When the mind has once begun to yield to the weakness of superstition, trifles impress it with the force of conviction.' (Ann Radcliffe, *The Mysteries of Udolpho*, 1764)

When once

'When once any object has been seen, it is impossible to put the mind back to the same condition it was in before it saw it.' (Thomas Paine, *The Rights of Man*, 1791)

While

'While I sat thus, looking at the fire, and seeing pictures in the red-hot coals, I almost believed that I had never been away; that Mr. and Miss Murdstone were such pictures, and would vanish when the fire got low; and that there was nothing real in all that I remembered, save my mother, Peggotty, and I.' (Charles Dickens, *David Copperfield*, 1850)

With this in mind

'With this in mind let the impartial inquirer sum up the instances of ill-treatment, and note the degree of ill-treatment proved in each instance, making fair allowance for the state of feeling, and then let him sum up the evidence on the other side, with the same allowance,' (*House of Commons Papers*, Volume 16, 1841)

'With this in mind, your patience will pardon what might otherwise seem wearisome and cumbersome.' (*The Insurance Times*, Volume 14, 1881)

With this intention

'With this intention, and with this intention alone, it called upon the interposition of Russia.' (William Cobbett, *Cobbett's Political Register*, Volume 8, 1805)

'With this intention, they may be dried in a similar manner, and even mixed, with hay; and, if properly kept free from moisture, they may be easily preserved throughout the winter.' (*The Domestic Encyclopaedia*, 1804)

9. THE ART OF EXAMPLE AND ILLUSTRATION

If the writer has been using concepts, ideas, or theories, it is often helpful to provide an *illustration* or an *example*. For this purpose we deploy words such as:

another point, as an illustration, chiefly, especially, first thing to remember, for example, for instance, for one thing, for this reason, frequently, important to realize, in detail, in fact, in general, in other words, in particular, in this case, indeed, like, issues to consider, markedly, must be remembered, namely, notably, point often overlooked, recalling, specifically, such as, surely, surprisingly, that is to say, taking into account, to be sure, to put it another way, to put it differently, to repeat, with reference to, with regard to, with this in mind.

Perhaps the most common words, used at the beginning, or within a sentence are *for example* or *for instance*. As this chapter indicates – in combination with the idea of *Art of the Supplementary* - the English language affords a wide range of options beyond the most commonly used formulaic conventions.

Examples of the Art of Example and Illustration

Another point

'We had another point to consider; the sufficiency of our special schools as now organized, for giving such a scientific education in the various professions as the credit and great interests of the country require.' (*The New-York Review*, Volume 7, 1840)

'Lastly, there is another point to consider, on which the whole question may ultimately be found to hinge; and that is, the mode of selecting and paying the Guardians.' (Robert Bermingham Clements, *The present Poverty of Ireland...* 1838)

'The powers have also another point to consider—the fatal effect which the success of the Americans will have upon the future action of our transatlantic cousins.' (*The Literary Digest*, Volume 16, 1898)

As an example

'As an example of a small farmers in the county of Stafford, we select that of Knollwall. [...] As an example of a middle-sized farmery on a clayey soil, we may refer to that of Newstead, in Staffordshire.' (John Claudius Loudon, *An Encyclopædia of Agriculture: Comprising the Theory and Practice...*, 1826)

'As an example of the various shapes of the eggs of insects, and of their natural as well as magnified size, we refer to those of the common slug...' (Ibid.)

As an illustration

'As an illustration of the size and quality of the timber that occupied the site of the large and flourishing town of Sydney about forty-five years ago, I may mention the following circumstance: — On the summit of the ridge...' (John Dunmore Lang, *An Historical and Statistical Account of New South Wales*, 1834)

' As an illustration of the connexion between algebra and geometry, it must always be valuable: but we suppose no one would think of making it the foundation of geometry.' (*Penny Cyclopaedia of the Society for the Diffusion of Useful Knowledge*, 1840)

'Take, as an illustration of my remarks, the state of effervescence into which our community was stirred a little more than a year since, by the success of Atlantic Steam Navigation.' (*Southern Literary Messenger*, 1839)

Chiefly

'The readers should be carried forward, not merely or chiefly by the mechanical impulse of curiosity, or by a restless desire to arrive at the final solution; but by the pleasurable activity of mind excited by the attractions of the journey itself.' (Coleridge, *Biographia Literaria*, 1817)

Especially

'This is especially true in Louisiana where higher soil temperatures and water content increase microbial activity.' (*Soil Survey*, 1923)

'Especially significant is the recommendation which this committee of physicians places at the beginning of its report –' (*Bulletin of the United States Bureau of Labor Statistics*, 1922)

First thing to remember

'The first thing to remember is that in all nature, either plant or animal life, each new production partakes of its ancestors. Not entirely from the one immediate ancestor, but made up from a few generations back.' (*Ohio State Board of Agriculture Annual Report*, 1891)

'The first thing to remember in platinum printing, then, is that dampness of the paper before, during, or after printing, is fatal to satisfactory prints.' (*The Photo Miniature*, 1912)

For example

'For example, there is a limit of size beyond which it is impossible to make a successful walking - machine, and beyond which, therefore, a walking animal can not exist.' (Joseph Le Conte, *The Problems of a Flying Machine*, 1889)

For instance

'For instance, in the above example the vernal equinox falls on the 10th of March, eleven days before the rule supposes it;' (Charles Hutton, *A Philosophical and Mathematical Dictionary*, 1815)

'It cannot, for instance, keep the equinox always fixed on the 21st of March, but it will vary between the 19th and the 23rd.' (Charles Hutton, *A Philosophical and Mathematical Dictionary*, 1815)

For one thing

'Young men make great mistakes in life; for one thing, they idealize love too much.' (Bejamin Jowett, 1817-1993)

For the purpose of

'The breaking up of a street, whenever it takes place, whether it be for the purpose of water, gas, sewers, or whatever it may be, is always an annoyance amounting to a nuisance.' (*The Law Journal*, 1869)

For the same reason

'For the same reason, we may leave out of consideration those backward states of society in which the race itself may be considered as in its nonage.' (J. S. Mill, *On Liberty*, 1859)

For this reason

'While he enjoyed liberty, the regent could not reckon his own power secure. For this reason, having by an artifice allured Maitland to Stirling, he employed Captain Crawford, one of his creatures, to accuse him of being accessory to the murder of the king; and under that pretence he was arrested and carried as a prisoner to Edinburgh.' (William Robertson, *The History of Scotland during the Reign of Queen Mary and of King James VI*, 1836)

'They aimed at bringing about a change in the religion, and a revolution in the government of the kingdom. For this reason they solicited the aid of the king of Spain, the avowed and zealous patron of popery in that age.' (William Robertson, *The History of Scotland during the Reign of Queen Mary and of King James VI*, 1836)

Frequently

'Very frequently it is found that faults of much structural importance and with throws of several hundred feet have been impotent to impress their presence upon the topography, whose local development was, in such instances, controlled by other structural elements.' (*U.S. Geological Survey Professional Paper*, 1904)

'Frequently it is found that the base is not parallel with the axis of the armature, sometimes to the extent that it is necessary to take a cut off the bottom of the motor feet in order to true them up.' (*Automotive Industries, the Automobile*, Volume 57, 1927)

Important to realize that

'It is important to realize that productivity, as measured by yields, is not the only consideration that determines the relative worth of a soil for growing crops.' (*Soil Survey*, 1913)

'It is important to realise that cholera poison is not a definite compound, like arsenic or strychnine, held in solution and equably diffused throughout the water, but a series of minute particles capable of almost infinite multiplication by fissiparous development (i.e. one particle divides into two, this enlarges, and again subdivides with marvellous rapidity).' (*People's Magazine: An Illustrated Miscellany for Family Reading*, 1869)

In detail

'It is just one of the Pall Mall club-houses transplanted to Manchester, and the fine square general mass will tend to improve and simplify provincial taste; but, in detail, it is not the most happy of Mr. Barry's works in what may be called that Greco-Italian style which is, I think, his fort.' (*Architectural Magazine, and Journal of Improvement in Architecture...*, Volume 5, 1838)

In fact

'In fact, it is a farce to call any being virtuous whose virtues do not result from the exercise of its own reason.' (Mary Wollstonecraft)

In general

'In general the accent is thrown as far back in polysyllables as the fourth and fifth syllables...' (Thomas Sheridan, *A General Dictionary of the English Language*, 1780)

In other words

'In other words, the *Barocco* manner had begun; the path was opened to prank, caprice, and license.' (John Addington Symonds, *The Life of Michelangelo Buonarroti*, Volume 2, p. 17)

' "She will be as well in a day or two," said Mr. Woodcourt, looking at her with an observant smile, "as she ever will be. In other words, quite well of course. Have you heard of her good fortune?" ' (Charles Dickens, *Bleak House*, 1852)

In particular

'To the first argument in particular, it is a farther answer, that it was the style of all the sacred writers, and it is the style of all writers, to name things rather after their appearances than their internal forms.' (Olinthus Gregory Letters on the Evidences, Doctrines, and Duties, of the Christian Religion, 1836)

'In particular, it is incumbent on the directors and rectors of gymnasia and town schools, to lake an active interest in the younger masters, to afford them advice, and to point out their errors, and to stimulate them to improve themselves by attending the lessons of more experienced teachers, by cultivating their society, by forming school conferences or other associations of instructors, and by studying the best works on education.' (Henry Barnard, Ed., *Connecticut Common School Journal*, 1839)

In this case

'Where the act, though not unintentional, is *unadvised,* insomuch that the mischievous part of the consequences is unintentional, but the unadvisedness is attended with *heedlessness*. In this case the act is attended with some small degree of secondary mischief, in proportion to the degree of heedlessness.' (Jeremy Bentham, *The Works of Jeremy Bentham*, 1838)

Indeed

'Indeed, there is much to be said in favour of the physical force of the public than there is in favour of the public's opinion. The former may be fine. The latter must be foolish.' (Wilde, *The Soul of Man*)

'Indeed I tremble for my country when I reflect that God is just.' (Thomas Jefferson)

Like

'It is a composition of a squirrel, a hare, a rat, and a monkey, which altogether looks very like a bird.' (Horace Walpole, *Letters*, 1752)

'A husband is a mere bugbear, a snap-dragon, a monster; that is to say, if one make him so, then he is a monster indeed; and if one do not make him so, then he behaves like a monster ; and of the two evils, by my troth [...]' (Arthur Murphy, *The Way to keep Him*, 1826)

'Who can read fairy tales like a child 1 Who can believe the tales of the Arabian Nights like a child? Who can fear haunted places like a child? Who can tremble at a ghost story like a child? Who can conjure up spirits in the dark like a child?' (Henry Ware, *A Discourse Preached at the Ordination of Mr. Robert C. Waterston*, 1840)

Like all

'Like all that I have written for many years, it belongs as much to her as to me [...]' (J. S. Mill, *On Liberty*, 1859)

'Like all men of genius, he delighted to take refuge in poetry from the vulgarity and irritation of business. His own verses were easy and pleasant, and might have claimed no low place among those, which the French call *vers de society*.' (Robert Huish, *Memoirs of George the Fourth*, 1830)

'Theologians, like all men who devote themselves to one special pursuit, not only lose sight of every thing else, but end by even forgetting the true end of their own reflections and researches.' (*The Monthly Chronicle*, Volume 4, 1839)

Issues to consider

'In studying an industry with a view to training its workers either before or after they have entered the industry, there are four important issues to consider:' (Charles Henry Winslow, *Conciliation, Arbitration, and Sanitation in the Dress and Waist Industry of New York City*, 1914)

Markedly

'It is not markedly an Italian work, therefore, but there is something of Italy in it; and one feels this mainly in the cosmopolitan manner which characterizes it, and which we began by speaking of.' (*The Atlantic Monthly*, 1890)

Must be remembered that

'Then, in the second place, it must be remembered that the physical effect of the compression has been shown to be chiefly displacement, and not any arrest of development.' (*The West Riding Lunatic Asylum Medical Reports*, 1871)

'If he spoke fiercely, savagely, it must be remembered that he spoke of a fierce and savage matter; if he used, and it may be abused, all the arts of oratory, it must be remembered that he was fighting for the honour, and it may be for the national life, of his country [...]' (*Good Words*, Volume 9, 1868)

Namely

'The next source of diagnosis — namely, the alternation of the stethoscopic signs of bronchial obstruction with the symptoms of laryngeal irritation — forms, when available, the most important and conclusive diagnostic.' (Robley Dunglison *Dunglison's American Medical Library*, 1837)

'How are the twenty-six States divided? Answer. Into four divisions, namely, the Eastern, the Middle, the Southern, and the Western.' (Richard Green Parker, *Questions in Geography*, 1842)

Notably

'Notably we have here not merely contractions of muscles, but combined and harmonized contractions in due sequence for a special purpose.' (Henry Maudsley, *Body and Mind*, 1871)

Point often overlooked

'Another point often overlooked is the time at which the young chicks are fed.' (*Journal of the Bath and West of England Society*, 1871)

'Another point, often overlooked, may be noted here. A knowledge of the chemical composition and. properties of the various minerals found in a given county may perchance prevent the agriculturist from passing by unheeded some of the best treasures of the earth.' (John Constable, *Agricultural Education*, 1863)

'In connexion with the functions of the nervous system, Dr. Day notices a point often overlooked by the physician in his diagnosis as to the amount of disease present in any organ, namely, *the insulation of the different organs* which exists in old age.' (*Dublin Quarterly Journal of Medical Science*, Volume 8, 1849)

Recalling the example

'Not without the conscious pride of patriotism I shall have to tell, that the conquering soldiers of Gettysburg and Richmond, recalling the example of their ancestors the conquerors of Yorktown, went back, when their work was done, to the farm, the work-shop, or to trade; that an assaulted but victorious Government disdained the cruel retributions of the scaffold, and acted with security on the principle that the causes of political crimes must be remedied, but the crimes themselves not avenged.' (*Harper's Magazine*, Volume 35, 1867)

Specifically

'Specifically, this volume presents statistics relative to the Negro race—growth by decades; geographical distribution in 1930 and changes in this distribution during the previous 10 years; movement to the North and to the cities; sex and age composition; marital condition; annual mortality and births in the registration area; school attendance and illiteracy; criminality insofar as this can be measured by the number of persons committed to State and Federal prisons and reformatories; number gainfully occupied; distribution according to occupation groups; ownership and value of homes; religious bodies and Sunday schools; retail business as conducted by Negro proprietors; farms, farm operators, and agricultural production.' (*Negroes in the United States 1920-32*, United States Bureau of Census, 1935)

Such

'Such a characterization, with its intimations of tristesse and hint of Freudian pathos, may at first glance seem grandiose.' (Terry Castle, *Masquerade and Civilization*, 1986: 99)

'-- Such appears to be the constitution of man.' (Mary Hays, *Memoirs of Emma Courtney*)

'Such was our domestic circle, from which care and pain seemed for ever banished.' (Mary Shelley, *Frankenstein: or, The modern Prometheus*, 1818)

Such are

'Such are the chief problems which I have solved, and which have never yet been submitted to calculation.' (Fourier, *Theory of Heat*)

'Such was the *nidus* or soil, which constituted, in the strict sense of the word, the circumstances of Milton's mind.' (Coleridge, Milton)

Such things

'Such things, as I say, were to come back to her—they played through her full after-sense like lights on the whole impression; the subsequent parts of the experience were not to have blurred their distinctness.' (Henry James, *The Golden Bowl*, 1904)

Surely

'Surely something resides in this heart that is not perishable - and life is more than a dream.' (Mary Wollstonecraft Shelley, *Letters*)

Surprisingly

'Surprisingly cheerful they generally are, and to witness them at work is very interesting.' (John Chilcott, *Chilcott's Descriptive History of Bristol*, 1840)

That is to say

'That is to say, I presume, that all would go wrong!' (Edward Bulwer Lytton Lytton, *New Monthly Magazine*, 1820)

'That is to say, you suppose them to oblige themselves to a general and extravagant fast from mere wantonness, and without any object whatever!' (Ibid.)

Take

'Take, for instance, the choice of synonyms.' (*The Popular Science Monthly*, 1885)

Taking into account

'I cannot say how they may be in England generally, but I can say that rents in the county of Cork, taking into account the condition of' the farms, are decidedly higher than the rents in Hampshire and Dorsetshire, taking into account the condition of the farms there.' (*Report from the Select Committee of the House of Lords on the Tenure (Ireland) Bill*, 1867)

'Taking into account that our fractional coin has a column in which even the ordinary principle of reducing fractions to a common denominator is not adopted, but you have two, and taking into account further that in the column of pence you have a different principle [...]' (*Decimal Coinage Commissioners: Preliminary Report*, 1857)

To be sure

'Well, I say nothing; but to be sure it is a pity some folks had not been better born; nay, as for that matter, I should not mind it myself; but then there is not so much money; and what of that?' (Henry Fielding, *Tom Jones*, 1749)

'To be sure it is natural for us to wish our enemies dead, that the wars may be at an end and our taxes be lowered; for it is a dreadful thing to pay as we do.' (Henry Fielding, *Tom Jones*, 1749)

'Well, to be sure, it is curious; but some such there have been, and always will be, in the gay world; and indeed they are very amusing; it is beyond belief how they divert one.' (Charlotte Campbell Bury, *Flirtation: a Novel*, 1827)

'To be sure, he has not a vital interest in the suit in question, her part in which was the only property my Lady brought him; and he has a shadowy impression that for his name—the name of Dedlock—to be in a cause, and not in the title of that cause, is a most ridiculous accident.' (Charles Dickens, *Bleak House*, 1852)

To put it another way

'To put it another way, what is the most important single aspect of training? In my opinion, it is the ability to diagnose learning difficulties, which will be different for different trainees, even though a standardized package is being presented.' (*Marketing Series*, 1841)

'Or to put it another way; a thought unspoken is a seed in the mould. By due culture it will flower into words.' (Oliver Bell Bunce, *A Bachelor's Story*, 1860)

To put it differently

'Or to put it differently, it is the test of the quantity of truth that there is in our favourite prejudices.' (William Hazlitt, *Lectures on the English Comic Writers*, 1819)

'Or, to put it differently, he teaches that the perfected man must be, like a compass-needle, delicately responsive to the currents that rule alike in matter and spirit; that he must be open to the influences of Nature and Humanity, and yet, following his proper genius, help on the ascending Creation by the divinity which is in him.' (Ralph Waldo Emerson, *The Conduct of Life*, 1860)

To repeat

'Ireland, we beg to repeat it, is an island gifted with an extraordinary range of coast, as compared with its acreable contents; and still further gifted in the equally extraordinary capabilities of that coast towards the nautical advantages of the empire.' (*The Dublin Review*, 1837)

'But I am sorry to repeat, it is impossible. Such a marriage would irretrievably blight my son's career, and ruin his prospects.' (Charles Dickens, *David Copperfield*, 1849)

With reference to

'With reference to the third request, the Sirdar Mahomed Akbar may be assured that I would guarantee his personal safety whenever he may visit my camp; but his doing so would require some preliminary arrangement, unless he voluntarily claims our protection, in which case I could immediately arrange for his safety, and appeal to the government on his behalf.' (Sir John William Kaye, *History of the War in Afghanistan*, Volume 3, 1858)

With regard to

'All this arises from a wrong bias given to the mind, in our course of education, with regard to two material articles. The first is, a total neglect of our own tongue, from the time and pains necessary to the attainment of two dead languages.' (Thomas Sheridan, *A Complete Dictionary of the English* Language, 1789)

'With regard to the first, it follows as a matter of course that, whenever we agree to any terms, amnesty for the past will result.' (Sir John William Kaye, *History of the War in Afghanistan*, Volume

3, 1858)

With this in mind

'With this in mind let the impartial inquirer sum up the instances of ill-treatment, and note the degree of ill-treatment proved in each instance, making fair allowance for the state of feeling, and then let him sum up the evidence on the other side, with the same allowance,' (*House of Commons Papers*, Volume 16, 1841)

'With this in mind, your patience will pardon what might otherwise seem wearisome and cumbersome.' (*The Insurance Times*, Volume 14, 1881)

10. THE ART OF THE SUMMARY

Having outlined their thoughts on a topic, writers often provide a *summary* of their ideas. In this regard useful connective words include:

after all, all in all, all things considered, by and large, finally, for the most part, generally speaking, hence, in a word, in any event, in brief, in conclusion, in conclusion, in essence, in fact, in short, in summary, in the final analysis, in the long run, on balance, on the whole, ordinarily, overall, that is to say, that is, to sum up, to summarize, usually.

If you are constructing an essay involving a strong argument remember that it is helpful to summarise your ideas at the end of a paragraph, and at the end of your essay.

As this chapter demonstrates, you are not obliged to stick to the tired formula, 'in conclusion …'

Examples of the Art of the Summary

After all

'After all, concentration is the price the modern student pays for success.' (William Osler, *The Student Life*, 1931)

'And, after all, it mattered very little to herself.' (Charles Dickens, *All the Year Round*, Volume 3, 1870)

'After all it was only the old story over again. Many have done the like before, many will do it yet.' (*All for the best, a Story of quiet Life*, 1861)

All in all

'All in all, long-term delinquency in the selected Wisconsin towns quite accurately mirrors economic conditions.' (Fred Rogers Fairchild, *Forest taxation in the United States*, United Statea Department of Agriculture, 1935)

'All in all, despite Prof. Gwillim's modest disclaimer, this is one of the best records that we have procured.' (*United States Geological Survey* 69, 1912)

All things considered

'But, all things considered, it is his pleasure that the wicked should die; for "the day of vengeance is in his heart."' (*The Volunteer*, 1832)

'This sir Isaac Newton finely improves on: "All things considered (says that great author), it appears probable to me, that God, in the beginning, created matter in solid, hard, impenetrable, moveable particles; of such sizes and figures, and with such other properties, as most conduced to the end for which he formed them [...]"' (*Pantologia: A New Cyclopaedia*, 1813)

By and large

'By and large, planning agencies have been responsible for the development of what are called metropolitan airport, or aircraft noise abatement policy studies, carried on by the Department of HUD, during the past 4 years.' (*Public Hearings on Noise Abatement and Control: Technology and economics of Noise Control*, United States. Office of Noise, 1971)

Finally

'Finally, I believe that many lowly organised forms now exist throughout the world, from various causes.' (Darwin, *The Origin of Species*, 1859)

'But finally they lost patience, seeing that their reformatory efforts went for nothing, and threw both friends and strangers overboard.' (Mark Twain, *What is Man? and Other Essays*, 1906)

'So they determined to cross to the other side and held councils to work out a plan by which the passage might be accomplished. Finally they decided that they must construct a raft.' (John Reed Swanton, *Chickasaw Society and Religion*, 1928)

'Finally, it may be useful to my readers to restate what this book does not set out to do.' (Mary Russo, *The Female Grotesque: Risk, Excess and Modernity*, 1994: 14)

For the most part

'And all this is, for the most part, that subtle kind of localism of which it is much easier to show the existence than to ascertain the cause.' (*The Ecclesiologist*, 1850)

'For the most part, the roads in the island are steps cut or laid in the solid rock; and our alert, sure-footed little animals, climbed them with the agility of mountain goats.' (*Southern Literary Messenger*, 1840)

Generally

'It is generally conceded that cases properly diagnosed as delirium tremens are rare, and usually occur in persons who lead a sedentary life, and are of nervous or sanguine temperament; and in those whose intemperate habits have been long confirmed, and uninterrupted by occasionally violent and unusual excesses.' (Albert Day, *Methomania: A treatise on Alcoholic Poisoning*, 1867)

General truth

'The general truth of the principle, long ago insisted on by Humboldt, that man admires and often tries to exaggerate whatever characters nature may have given him, is shown in many ways.' (Charles Darwin, *The Descent of Man*)

Generally speaking

'Generally speaking, up until about twenty years ago, historians of this period usually thought of *the* Enlightenment, as a relatively unitary phenomenon in the history of ideas...' (Dorinda Outram, *The Enlightenment*, 1995: 3)

Hence

'Hence, the struggle for the production of new and modified descendents will mainly lie between larger groups which are all trying to increase in number.' (Charles Darwin, *The Origin of Species*, 1859)

'Hence, perhaps, the peculiar nature of woman in fiction; the astonishing extremes of her beauty and horror; her alternations between heavenly goodness and hellish depravity — for so a lover would see her as his love rose or sank, was prosperous or unhappy.' (Virginia Woolf, *A Room of One's Own*, 1929)

In a word

'In a word, those who do good from the former origin, do it not from any conscience of what is just and equitable, still less from a conscience of spiritual truth and good: but those who do good from the other origin, do it from conscience;'

(Emanuel Swedenborg, *Arcana cœlestia: or Heavenly mysteries contained in the sacred Scriptures*, 1863)

'In a word, he was ready to shew, that those who could, after such a full and fair exposure, continue to countenance the French insanity, were not mistaken politicians, but bad men; but he thought that in this case, as in many others, ignorance had been the cause of admiration.' (Edmund Burke, *The Works of Edmund Burke*, Volume 3, 1839)

In any event

'In any event, I am persuaded that we shall place no reliance on a declared enemy; and that, if the aid to which we are entitled is withheld, the means which God has given us will be faithfully employed for our safety.' (Theodore Dwight, *The History of Connecticut: From the First Settlement to the Present Time*, 1840)

'In any event, this will be a harmless measure, as it can operate only upon those who voluntarily assent to it.' (*The Congressional Globe*, 1839)

In brief

'In brief, then, if the cause is matter, the effect is matter; if the cause is a force, the effect is also a force.' (*The Correlation and Conservation of Forces: a Series of Expositions*, 1865)

'They have, in brief, all the light, unenviable qualities of Eastern women. They excel in finesse.' (Frank Fowler, *Southern Lights and*

Shadows: being Brief Notes of Three Years' Experience of Social, Literary and Political Life in Australia..., 1859)

'In, brief, the wrong which Scott and Constable did each other, was a mutual wrong. Each was alike willing to be flatteringly deceived, and Scott, in the first instance, had the pecuniary advantage, and used it.' (*Tait's Edinburgh Magazine*, 1838)

In conclusion

'In conclusion, it is hoped that in the present paper such a mixture of courtesy and of dissent, free from personal satire, has prevailed, as may be deemed fitting for the occasion, especially as such elements are of all others the most easy to be departed from.' (*Journal of the Institute of Actuaries*, Volume 3, 1853)

In essence

'In essence, policymakers have learned how to better manage monetary policy over the past two decades.' (*Congressional Budget Office*, 2006)

'In essence, the Disclosure Statement submitted by the contractor, by distinguishing between direct and indirect costs.' (*Office of the Federal Register*, 1975)

In fact

'In fact, it is a farce to call any being virtuous whose virtues do not result from the exercise of its own reason.' (Mary Wollstonecraft)

In short

'In short, he became so absorbed in his books that he spent his nights from sunset to sunrise, and his days from dawn to dark, poring over them; and what with little sleep and much reading his brains got so dry that he lost his wits.' (Cervantes, *Don Quixote*, 1605)

In some cases

'In some cases variations or individual differences of a favourable nature may never have arisen for natural selection to act on and accumulate.' (Darwin, *The Origin of Species*, 1859)

In some few cases

'In some few cases there has been what we must call retrogression of organisation.' (Darwin, *The Origin of Species*, 1859)

In summary

'In summary, it is the writer's opinion that Stenomyelon is closely related to various calamopityean genera and should be assigned to the family Calamopityeae.' (*United States Geological Survey Professional Paper*, 1902)

In the final analysis

'In the final analysis, we find that Walton's book is interesting mainly because it is a picture of himself.' (*Oberlin Students' Monthly*, 1858)

'In the final analysis, however, the planner is providing recommendations that he or she may have little if any control in implementing.' (*Micromanpower Planning in the Public Sector*, 1974)

'In the final analysis, complete coordination may not be achievable.' (*US Army: Co-ordinated Power Systems Protection*, 1991)

In the long run

'In the long run the Texans had the best of it, and the Mexicans found the land north of the Rio Grande untenable.' (Walter Prescott Webb, *The Great Plains*, 1931)

'None, in the long run, will suffer but the selfish aristocrats who have hitherto saved themselves from insolvency by levying an enormous tax upon the other classes of the community.' (*Blackwood's Magazine*, 1838)

'In the long run, those who obey become accustomed to the yoke; the sword is drawn, and the factious are hurled to the dust.' (*Literary Gazette*, 1820)

On balance

'On balance, it is our view that the arguments against the enactment of S. 11 substantially outweigh those favoring such enactment.' (*U. S. Senate Hearings*, 1857)

On the whole

'On the whole, an artist in England gains something by being attacked. His individuality is intensified. He becomes more completely himself.' (Wilde, *The Soul of Man*)

Ordinarily

'Ordinarily we adapt to the extremity of the syphon tubes, a strip of linen divided into bandalets which serve not only to direct the liquid, but principally to obviate its dynamic effect.' (Stephen

Smith, *Hand-Book of Surgical Operations*, 1862)

That is to say

That is to say, I presume, that all would go wrong! (Edward Bulwer Lytton, *New Monthly Magazine*, 1820)

That is to say, you suppose them to oblige themselves to a general and extravagant fast from mere wantonness, and without any object whatever! (Ibid.)

To summarize

'To summarize, we quote that part of her testimony in connection with the immediate act of stabbing, as follows:' (*The Southwestern Reporter*, 1808)

'To illustrate: Two parties are seen engaged in an altercation. One draws a pistol, and fires at his adversary, standing some 10 or 15 steps distant.' (*The Southwestern Reporter*, 1808)

'Where the court in a trial for murder gives no instruction on provocation, or the bringing on of an assault by defendant, it is not error to refuse an instruction asked by defendant on that subject.' (*The Southwestern Reporter*, 1808)

To sum up

'To sum up all; there are archives at every stage to be looked into, and rolls, records, documents, and endless genealogies, which justice ever and anon calls him back to stay the reading of: in short, there is no end of it.' (Laurence Sterne, *The Life and Opinions of Tristram Shandy, Gentleman*, 1759)

Usually

'The wadding, if firm, may cause a mortal wound: usually it is intercepted by the dress, but now and then it penetrates to a short distance, and remains in the wound.' (*The Medical Examiner: A Monthly Record of Medical Science*, 1840)

'Parrots will often pick up words, or odds and ends of sentences; but usually it is desired that they shall learn some particular phrases, to suit the fancy of their owner.' (Maturin Murray Ballou, *Ballou's Monthly Magazine*, Volume 30, 1869)

11. FURTHER READING

Amidon, Arlene. "Children's understanding of sentences with contingent relations: Why are temporal and conditional connectives so difficult?" *Journal of Experimental Child Psychology* 22.3 (1976): 423-437.

Astington, Janet Wilde, Janette Pelletier, and Bruce Homer. "Theory of mind and epistemological development: The relation between children's second-order false-belief understanding and their ability to reason about evidence." *New Ideas in Psychology* 20.2 (2002): 131-144.

Bakewell, Sarah. *How to Live: A Life of Montaigne in one question and twenty attempts at an answer.* Vintage, 2011.

Baker, Linda. "Comprehension monitoring: Identifying and coping with text confusions." *Journal of Literacy Research* 11.4 (1979): 365-374.

Bates, Elisabeth, Philip S. Dale, and Donna Thal. "Individual differences and their implications for theories of language development." *The Handbook of Child Language* (1995): 96-151.

Beilin, Harry, and Barbara Lust. "A study of the development of logical and linguistics connectives: Linguistics data." *Studies in the cognitive basis of language development* (1975): 76-120.

Bizzell, Patricia, and Bruce Herzberg, eds., *The rhetorical tradition: Readings from classical times to the present*. Boston, MA: Bedford Books of St. Martin's Press, 1990.

Bloom, Lois, et al. "Complex sentences: Acquisition of syntactic connectives and the semantic relations they encode." *Journal of child language* 7.02 (1980): 235-261.

Bloom, Lois. *Language development from two to three*. Cambridge University Press, (1993).

Bondi, Marina. "Connectives." *The Encyclopedia of Applied Linguistics*.

Braine, Martin, and Barbara Rumain. "Logical reasoning." *Handbook of child psychology* 3 (1983): 263-340.

Braunwald, Susan R. "The development of connectives." *Journal of pragmatics* 9.4 (1985): 513-525.

Braunwald, Susan R. "The development of because and so: Connecting language, thought, and social understanding." *Studies in the production and comprehension of text*, Mahwah (NJ): Lawrence Erlbaum Assoc (1997): 121-137.

Brostoff, Anita. "Coherence:" Next to" Is Not" Connected to"." *College composition and communication* 32.3 (1981): 278-294.

Byrnes, James P., and Willis F. Overton. "Reasoning about logical connectives: A developmental analysis." *Journal of Experimental Child Psychology* 46.2 (1988): 194-218.

Clancy, Patricia, T. Iacobsen, and Marilyn Silva. *The Acquisition of Conjunction: A Cross-Linguistic Study. Papers and Reports on Child Language Development*. ERIC Clearinghouse, 1976.

Clark, Eve V. *First language acquisition*. Cambridge University Press, 2009.

Crewe, William J. "The illogic of logical connectives." *ELT journal*

44.4 (1990): 316-325.

Crowhurst, Marion. "Cohesion in argument and narration at three grade levels." *Research in the Teaching of English* (1987): 185-201.

Crusius, Timothy W., and Carolyn E. Channell. *The aims of argument: A rhetoric and reader*. Mayfield Publishing Company, 1998.

Cudd, Evelyn T., and Leslie Roberts. "Using writing to enhance content area learning in the primary grades." *The Reading Teacher* 42.6 (1989): 392-404.

Davies, Peter, Becky Shanks, and Karen Davies. "Improving narrative skills in young children with delayed language development." *Educational Review* 56.3 (2004): 271-286.

Degand, Liesbeth, Nathalie Lefèvre, and Yves Bestgen. "The impact of connectives and anaphoric expressions on expository discourse comprehension." *Document Design* 1.1 (1999): 39-51.

Deleuze, Gilles, and Félix Guattari. *Capitalisme et schizophrénie*. Vol. 1. Les Editions de minuit, 1972.

Deleuze, Gilles, and Felix Guattari. *Anti-oedipus*. Continuum International Publishing Group, 2004.

Deleuze, Gilles, and Felix Guattari. *A thousand plateaus*. Trans. Brian Massumi. Minneapolis: University of Minnesota Press, 1987.

Derrida, Jacques. *Dissemination*. Continuum International Publishing Group, 2004.

Dickens, Charles. *A Tale of Two Cities* (1859).

Doyle, Walter, and Kathy Carter. "Academic tasks in classrooms." *Curriculum Inquiry* 14.2 (1984): 129-149.

Dubin, Fraida, and Elite Olshtain. "The interface of writing and reading." *TESOL Quarterly* (1980): 353-363.

Emerson, Harriet F., and William L. Gekoski. "Development of comprehension of sentences with "because" or "if"." *Journal of Experimental Child Psychology* 29.2 (1980): 202-224.

Fahnestock, Jeanne. "Semantic and lexical coherence." *College composition and communication* 34.4 (1983): 400-416.

Falmagne, Rachel J. "Language and the acquisition of logical knowledge." *Reasoning, necessity, and logic: Developmental perspectives* (1990): 111-131.

Forster, E.M. *Howards End.* 1910.

Freedman, Sarah W. "How characteristics of student essays influence teachers' evaluations." *Journal of Educational Psychology* 71.3 (1979): 328.

Gajdusek, Linda. "Toward wider use of literature in ESL: Why and how." *Tesol Quarterly* 22.2 (1988): 227-257.

Gardner, P. L. "The identification of specific difficulties with logical connectives in science among secondary school students." *Journal of Research in Science Teaching* 17.3 (1980): 223-229.

Gillet, Andy, Angela Hammond and Mary Martala, *Successful Academic Writing*, Pearson Education, 2009.

Goldman, Susan R., and John D. Murray. "Knowledge of connectors as cohesion devices in text: A comparative study of native-English and English-as-a-second-language speakers." *Journal of Educational Psychology* 84.4 (1992): 504.

Griffiths, Toni, and David Guile. "A connective model of learning: the implications for work process knowledge." *European educational research journal* 2.1 (2003): 56-73.

Grout, Edward H., *Standard English: Structure and Style.* Pitman, 1933.

Hamilton, William, *Lectures on Metaphysics.* 2 vols, 1860.

Hatch, Evelyn. "The young child's comprehension of time connectives." *Child Development* (1971): 2111-2113.

Hazlitt, William. 'Essay On Good Nature.' 1816.

Hobbes, Thomas. *The Elements of Law Natural and Politic.* 1640.

Hood, Lois, Lois Bloom, and Charles J. Brainerd. "What, when, and how about why: A longitudinal study of early expressions of causality." *Monographs of the Society for Research in Child Development* (1979): 1-47.

Horn, Vivian. "One Way to Read a Paragraph." *Elementary English* 50.6 (1973): 871-874.

Humberstone, Lloyd, *The Connectives*. Cambridge, MA: MIT Press, 2011

Jennings, R. E. "The meanings of connectives." *Davis & Gillon* (2004).

Johnson, Barbara. *The critical difference: Essays in the contemporary rhetoric of reading.* JHU Press, 1985.

Joyce, James. *Ulysses.* (1922):

Kahane, Howard, and Nancy Cavender. *Logic and contemporary rhetoric: The use of reason in everyday life.* CengageBrain.com, 2006.

Kames, Lord. *Elements of Criticism* (1762).

Katz, E. Walker and Sandor B. Brent. "Understanding connectives." *Journal of Verbal Learning and Verbal Behavior* 7.2 (1968): 501-509.

Kidd, Evan, and Edith L. Bavin. "English-speaking children's comprehension of relative clauses: Evidence for general-cognitive and language-specific constraints on development." *Journal of Psycholinguistic Research* 31.6 (2002): 599-617.

Kiniry, Malcolm, and Ellen Strenski. "Sequencing expository writing: A recursive approach." *College Composition and Communication* 36.2 (1985): 191-202.

Lenker, Ursula, and Anneli Meurman-Solin, eds. *Connectives in the*

History of English: Selected Papers from 13th ICEHL, Vienna, 23-28 August 2004).. Vol. 283. John Benjamins Publishing, 2007.

Lucas, F. L., *Style*. Cassell, 1955.

Lust, Barbara, Yu-Chin Chien, and Suzanne Flynn. "What children know: Methods for the study of first language acquisition." *Studies in the acquisition of anaphora*. Springer Netherlands, 1987. 271-356.

Maat, Henk Pander, and Ted Sanders. "Subjectivity in causal connectives: An empirical study of language in use." *Cognitive Linguistics* 12.3 (2001): 247-274.

Markels, Robin Bell. "Cohesion paradigms in paragraphs." *College English* 45.5 (1983): 450-464.

Maury, Pascale, and Amelie Teisserenc. "The role of connectives in science text comprehension and memory." *Language and Cognitive Processes* 20.3 (2005): 489-512.

MacArthur, Charles A., and Leah Lembo. "Strategy instruction in writing for adult literacy learners." *Reading and Writing* 22.9 (2009): 1021-1039.

Mason, Linda H., Richard M. Kubina, and Raol J. Taft. "Developing quick writing skills of middle school students with disabilities." *The Journal of Special Education* 44.4 (2011): 205-220.

Mellor, Anne K., *English Romantic Irony*. Harvard University Press, 1990.

McClure, Erica, and Esther Geva. "The development of the cohesive use of adversative conjunctions in discourse." *Discourse processes* 6.4 (1983): 411-432.

McCutchen, Deborah. "From novice to expert: Implications of language skills and writing-relevant knowledge for memory during the development of writing skill." *Journal of Writing Research* 3.1 (2011): 51-68.

Millis, Keith K., and Marcel Adam Just. "The influence of

connectives on sentence comprehension." *Journal of Memory and Language* 33.1 (1994): 128-147.

Miltsakaki, Eleni, et al. "Annotating discourse connectives and their arguments." *Proceedings of the HLT/NAACL Workshop on Frontiers in Corpus Annotation.* 2004.

Morris, Bradley J. "Logically speaking: Evidence for item-based acquisition of the connectives AND & OR." *Journal of Cognition and Development* 9.1 (2008): 67-88.

Müller, Ulrich, Bryan Sokol, and Willis F. Overton. "Developmental sequences in class reasoning and propositional reasoning." *Journal of Experimental Child Psychology* 74.2 (1999): 69-106.

Murray, John D. "Logical connectives and local coherence." *Sources of coherence in reading* (1995): 107-125.

Murray, John D. "Connectives and narrative text: The role of continuity." *Memory & Cognition* 25.2 (1997): 227-236.

Myers, Jerome L., Makiko Shinjo, and Susan A. Duffy. "Degree of causal relatedness and memory." *Journal of Memory and Language* 26.4 (1987): 453-465.

Neimark, Edith D., and Nan S. Slotnick. "Development of the understanding of logical connectives." *Journal of Educational Psychology* 61.6p1 (1970): 451.

Neuwirth, Sharyn E. "A look at intersentence grammar." *The Reading Teacher* 30.1 (1976): 28-32.

Nippold, Marilyn A., Ilsa E. Schwarz, and Robin A. Undlin. "Use and understanding of adverbial conjuncts: a developmental study of adolescents and young adults." *Journal of Speech, Language and Hearing Research* 35.1 (1992): 108.

Paribakht, T. Sima, and Marjorie Bingham Wesche. "Reading comprehension and second language development in a comprehension-based ESL program." *TESL Canada journal* 11.1

(1993): 09-29.

Paris, Scott G. "Comprehension of language connectives and propositional logical relationships." *Journal of experimental child psychology* 16.2 (1973): 278-291.

Perelman, Chaim, and Carroll C. Arnold. *The realm of rhetoric.* Notre Dame, IN: University of Notre Dame Press, 1982.

Peterson, Carole, and Allyssa McCabe. "Linking children's connective use and narrative macrostructure." *Developing narrative structure* (1991): 29-53.

Peterson, Carole and A. McCabe. "A naturalistic study of the production of causal connectives by children." *Journal of Child Language* 12 (1985): 145-159.

Peterson, Carole, and Allyssa McCabe. "The connective 'and': Do older children use it less as they learn other connectives." *Journal of Child Language* 14.02 (1987): 375-381.

Peterson, Carole, and Allyssa McCabe. "The connective and as discourse glue." *First Language* 8.22 (1988): 19-28.

Platts, Mark de Bretton. *Ways of meaning: An introduction to a philosophy of language.* MIT Press, 1997.

Pope, Alexander. *Essay on Criticism.* 1711.

Posner, Roland. "Semantics and pragmatics of sentence connectives in natural language." *Speech act theory and pragmatics.* Springer Netherlands, 1980. 169-203.

Raban, Bridie. "Speaking and writing: Young children's use of connectives." *Child Language Teaching and Therapy* 4.1 (1988): 13-25.

Rickards, Debbie, and Shirl Hawes. "Connecting reading and writing through author's craft." *The Reading Teacher* 60.4 (2006): 370-373.

Robertson, Jean E. "Pupil understanding of connectives in reading." *Reading Research Quarterly* (1968): 387-417.

Sams, Lynn. "How to teach grammar, analytical thinking, and writing: A method that works." *The English Journal* 92.3 (2003): 57-65.

Sanders, Ted. "Coherence, causality and cognitive complexity in discourse." *Proceedings/Actes SEM-05, First International Symposium on the exploration and modelling of meaning*. 2005.

Silva, Marilyn N. "Perception and the choice of language in oral narrative: the case of the co-temporal connectives." *Proceedings of the Annual Meeting of the Berkeley Linguistics Society*. Vol. 7. 2011.

Sinatra, Richard, et al. "Combining visual literacy, text understanding, and writing for culturally diverse students." *Journal of Reading* 33.8 (1990): 612-617.

Sinatra, Richard C. "Teaching learners to think, read, and write more effectively in content subjects." *The Clearing House* 73.5 (2000): 266-273.

Snow, Catherine E., and Paola Uccelli. "The challenge of academic language." *The Cambridge handbook of literacy* (2009): 112-133.

Spooren, Wilbert. "The processing of underspecified coherence relations." *Discourse processes* 24.1 (1997): 149-168.

Steiner, George. *Grammars of creation: originating in the Gifford lectures for 1990*. Yale University Press, 2002.

Stenning, Keith, and Lynn Michell. "Learning how to tell a good story: The development of content and language in children's telling of one tale." *Discourse Processes* 8.3 (1985): 261-279.

Sternberg, Robert J. "Developmental patterns in the encoding and combination of logical connectives." *Journal of Experimental Child Psychology* 28.3 (1979): 469-498.

Sterne, Laurence. *The Life and Opinions of Tristram Shandy, Gentleman*. 1759-67.

Stotsky, Sandra L. "Sentence-combining as a curricular activity: its effect on written language development and reading comprehension." *Research in the Teaching of English* 9.1 (1975): 30-71.

Stott, Rebecca and Simon Avery, eds., *Writing with Style*. Pearson Education Ltd 2001.

Stott, Rebecca and Kim Landers, 'Structures beyond the Sentence' in *Grammar and Writing*, eds., Rebecca Stott and Peter Chapman. Pearson Education Ltd, 2001.

Sullivan, Laraine. "Development of causal connectives by children." *Perceptual and Motor Skills* 35.3 (1972): 1003-1010.

Swift, Jonathan. *Gulliver's Travels*. 1726.

Susser, Bernard. "Process approaches in ESL/EFL writing instruction." *Journal of Second Language Writing* 3.1 (1994): 31-47.

Traill, H. D., 'Critical Introduction. Laurence Sterne' in *English Prose. Vol. IV. Eighteenth Century*, ed. Henry Craik, 1916.

Van Veen, Rosie, et al. "Parental input and connective acquisition: A growth curve analysis." *First Language* 29.3 (2009): 266-288.

Van Dijk, Teun A. "Pragmatic connectives." *Journal of pragmatics* 3.5 (1979): 447-456.

Van Eemeren, Frans H., et al. *Fundamentals of argumentation theory: A handbook of historical backgrounds and contemporary developments*. Mahwah, NJ: Lawrence Erlbaum Associates, 1996.

Wallace, David L., and John R. Hayes. "Redefining revision for freshmen." *Research in the Teaching of English* (1991): 54-66.

Wilkins, John. *An Essay towards a Real Character and a Philosophical Language*. 1668.

Wilkinson, Andrew. *The Foundations of Language; Talking and Reading to Young Children*. Oxford University Press, 1971.

ABOUT THE AUTHOR

Dr Ian McCormick served as a Professor at the University of Northampton until 2009. He holds degrees in English Language and Literature from the University of St Andrews (M.A.) and the University of Leeds (Ph.D).

Ian's postgraduate work was in the field of English literature and cultural history in the eighteenth century. He has also published and edited books on Gothic literature and Romanticism; John Dryden and T. S. Eliot; sexuality and gender studies; Robert Graves and modern literature; the contemporary Scottish novel; teaching and learning strategies; drama education; and literary, critical and cultural theory.

Ian's published work has been featured on the BBC Radio and TV, in the *Times Literary Supplement, The Observer, The Guardian, TimeOut* (London), and in many academic journals. Awards and Prizes include the King James VI Prize (1989); the Lawson Memorial Prize (1985); and the British Academy Major State Research Studentship (1990-93) which enabled him to pursue his doctoral research at the University of Leeds.

At present Ian works as an academic tutor and writer in Birmingham. His specialist work is in the field of language, education, creativity and participatory methodology. He also enjoys reading literary fiction, and writing about disability, the monstrous and the grotesque. He is currently working on a new book about Shakespearean tragedy.

Follow Ian on Twitter @postfilm.

http://english-skills-success.blogspot.co.uk/

Printed in Poland
by Amazon Fulfillment
Poland Sp. z o.o., Wrocław